Clematis

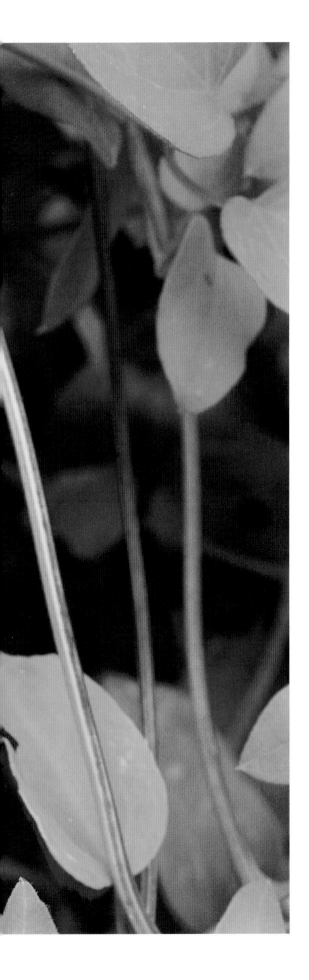

The Royal Horticultural Society

Clematis

Inspiration, selection and practical guidance

Charles Chesshire

Special photography
Andrew Lawson

Quadrille

Editorial Director Jane O'Shea
Art Director Helen Lewis
Project Editor Carole McGlynn
Art Editor Paul Welti
Photography Andrew Lawson, Sarah Cuttle
Production Rebecca Short, Vincent Smith

First published in 2004 by Quadrille Publishing
Limited

Half title (page 1): *Clematis* 'Tapestry'; Title page
(pages 2–3): *Clematis* 'Duchess of Albany'; this page
(right): *Clematis* 'Annemieke'

Clematis names

The naming of all clematis species and cultivars
published in this book follows the International
Clematis Register and Checklist 2002. Names for
cultivated varieties (cultivars) are printed in Roman
type and enclosed between single quotations, for
example 'Lasurstern'. Some plants have selling names
(properly known as trade designations), chosen to
attract sales when they are released into the trade.
Each trade designation must be registered with a
proper cultivar name but, as this is often a code or
nonsense word, the designated trade name is given
preference throughout this book. Where trade
designations are used, they are written in Roman
type, without quotation marks, for example
Arctic Queen. Cultivar names are linked to
designated trade names in the index, for example
Arctic Queen ('Evitwo').

Where a clematis has **AGM** after its name, it has been
given the Royal Horticultural Society's Award of
Garden Merit. To achieve this, its display must
represent good value in the garden and it should be
easy to care for, readily available and not especially
prone to pests and diseases.

contents

the
clematis
story

Although there are nearly 300 recorded species of *Clematis* known today, the genus did not feature in ancient literature or poetry and little is known about its first introduction into gardens in the sixteenth century. Despite the fact that clematis can boast no romantic past, these diverse climbers are now considered among the most beautiful and popular of all garden plants. Had the lovely Oriental species sent to Europe in the nineteenth century appeared in earlier times, no doubt they would, like the rose and the lily, have become the subjects of poets and painters.

C. texensis *(left) revolutionized the future of clematis hybridizing (see pages 12–13).*

early history

The earliest references to clematis appeared in botanical herbals dating from the 1500s and 1600s. The first of these were to the European species, especially *Clematis vitalba* or 'old man's beard', the rampant hedge vine whose fluffy

seedheads hold on deep into winter, when hoary ice encrusts the silvery seedheads. This vigorous species is unlikely to have been used much as a garden plant, although John Gerard says that it is 'esteemed by reason of its goodly shadow and the pleasant scent or savour of its flowers'.

In his *Herball* of 1636, John Gerard refers to *C. vitalba* as *Viorna, quasi vias ornus*, which he translated as 'of decking and adorning waies and hedges, where people travel; and thereupon I have named it the Traveller's Joy'. The old genus name of *Viorna* is now given to a group of clematis bearing urn-shaped flowers, most of which are native to North America. The plant was also known for some time under the genus name of *Atragene*, meaning 'firecracker' in Ancient Greek, for the noise the twigs make when burning. The name 'atragene' is now dedicated to the early-flowering group that includes *C. alpina* and *C. macropetala* which carry small, nodding, bell-shaped flowers. The more modern genus name of *Clematis* also comes from an Ancient Greek word, 'Klema', which simply means vine-like. This genus now encompasses a vast and varied group of plants that can be found growing wild in every continent of the world.

C. viticella *(left), known in cultivation since the 1500s, has had possibly the greatest influence on clematis breeding. It grows wild in central Europe and shares its qualities of hardiness, vigour, late flowering and purple-blue flowers with hundreds of cultivars.*

THE EUROPEAN SPECIES

From the mid-1500s to the end of the century, five other European species were introduced into cultivation. The most important of these was the vigorous and hardy *C. viticella*, introduced from south-eastern Europe in 1569. With its nodding purple flowers in late summer, *C. viticella* has come to lend its generous characteristics to many hybrids right into the twenty-first century. Gerard mentions *C. viticella* and its double-flowered form growing in his London garden in Holborn as early as 1597, 'where they flourish exceedingly'.

Four further species were introduced into cultivation during the course of the sixteenth century. *C. cirrhosa*, a winter-flowering evergreen with cream-coloured bells with freckled insides, is probably the true 'virgin's bower'; it hails

Cultivated ever since the sixteenth century, C. flammula (above) is a Mediterranean species which needs a dry, sunny spot. Often grown from seed commercially, it can be variable in the quality of its small white flowers and the intensity of its scent. It grows to 5m but is generally rather short-lived, especially if given a rich soil.

C. vitalba (opposite), known as old man's beard, is the rampant hedge vine whose fluffy seedheads hold on deep into winter. It is a familiar sight throughout Europe, especially in chalky areas.

from the Mediterranean and was discovered in Andalucia by the botanist Clusius. Also from the Mediterranean region and eastwards as far as Iran and the Caucasus comes *C. flammula*. In Provence in late summer whole hillsides of cistus, rosemary and scrub oak can be seen covered by its clouds of small, almond-scented flowers. In the Adriatic, I have seen *C. flammula* growing in dry stony soils, happily tumbling among the rocks and grasses.

C. recta was introduced into Britain in 1597 from northern Spain and eastwards into Europe and Russia. This species is strictly herbaceous, with most forms being so lanky that when they encounter the fertility and moisture of our gardens they tend to collapse unless they are very well-staked. *C. integrifolia*, another floppy herbaceous plant from eastern and central Europe and as far east as parts of China, has intriguing twisted bells of purple-blue. These two rather ungainly species may be seen in their native habitat growing on screes and on the edge of woodlands.

Both *C. viticella* and *C. integrifolia* are now being widely used in breeding for their hardiness and dwarf habit, as well, of course, as for their beauty. They may well have been the first clematis to be used in hybridization.

EARLY HYBRIDS

During the nineteenth century a flurry of breeding activity took place which eventually led to the introduction of hundreds of new clematis. It centred, initially, around the four European species introduced into Britain in the sixteenth century. The first known of these hybrids, produced in 1830, was *C. × eriostemon*, still in cultivation today but now also know as *C. × diversifolia*, with its hanging purple flowers midway between those of its parents, *C. integrifolia* and *C. viticella*.

Following the success of this hybrid, in 1857 *C. integrifolia* was crossed with *C. flammula* to produce *C. × aromatica*, a bushy plant bearing scented purple-blue flowers with prominent cream stamens. And in 1863 *C. viticella* was crossed with *C. flammula* to produce *C. × triternata* 'Rubromarginata', a larger plant also covered in fragrant starry flowers of purple and white.

THE ORIENTAL SPECIES

The real explosion of clematis hybrids happened in Europe during the second half of the nineteenth century and was due to the dramatic introduction of new species from the Orient. In particular, the three large-flowered species, *C. florida*, *C. patens* and *C. lanuginosa*, were to cause a sensation.

In 1853, after over 200 years of strict isolation, Japan was forced to open up its trade links with the rest of the world. Until then only a small enclave of Dutch traders off Nagasaki had been allowed any contact with Japanese culture or plants. Among them was the great Dutch botanist Dr von Siebold, who had assembled in his garden a remarkable plant collection and had published a book called *Flora Japonica*. To Dr von Siebold is attributed the introduction of *C. florida* into Europe in 1837 (although a plant exhibiting a double form of *C. florida* had been introduced to Sweden by Carl Thunberg as early as 1776).

There is much confusion about this plant and its origins, especially as it was thought to be virtually extinct in its native China by that time. The wild form has five or six creamy white sepals surrounding a boss of rich violet-purple stamens. At around the same time, Dr von Siebold sent to Europe some plants of *C. patens*, a variable species that bears the closest resemblance to modern large-flowered hybrids. This beautiful clematis has six to eight sepals in shades that vary from white, through pale mauve-pink to blue. The stamens are often a reddish purple but may equally be creamy yellow. It can still be found growing wild in parts of China, Korea and Japan.

When the British plant collector Robert Fortune visited Japan and China in 1863, he met Dr von Siebold, who appeared to be 'quite a prince amongst the people in this part of Japan'. Fortune brought back many cultivars of *C. patens*, including a fully double form which he named 'Fortunei', and 'Standishii', which was probably an old Japanese variety, both now extinct. In China he discovered another species, *C. lanuginosa*, 'near the city of Ningpo. It is there wild on the hill-sides, and generally plants itself in light

The original species may now be extinct in the wild, but the single form of C. florida *has recently come back into cultivation, mostly as seedlings from reversions of* C. florida *var.* sieboldiana. *These seedlings are again being used in the creation of new hybrids, 170 years after the species' first introduction from Japan.*

The hybridized form of C. florida, *var.* sieboldiana *is a fabulous plant with an exaggerated boss of distorted purple stamens that often cause it to be mistaken for a passion flower.*

stony soil near the roots of dwarf shrubs, whose stems furnish it with support as it grows . . . its fine, star-shaped azure blossoms . . . rearing themselves proudly above the shrubs.' Similar to *C. patens*, it was distinguished from it by overlapping sepals and by being a much hairier and stockier plant, with a longer flowering season. After seeing azaleas, which he had been sent to find, Fortune wrote that 'nor is it the azalea alone which claims our admiration; clematises, and a hundred others, mingle their flowers with them, and make us confess that China is indeed the "central flowery land".'

As with *C. florida*, it is doubtful whether *C. lanuginosa* now exists in the wild and it seems to be lost to cultivation, too. Doubts as to its true identity are fuelled by the probability that the Japanese had themselves been raising new varieties for over 200 years before the Europeans, and possibly the Chinese before them. It is now most likely that even the few remaining pockets of wild *C. patens* in Japan have lost their purity by having pollen carried into their populations from garden hybrids. Some experts doubt whether *C. patens* is even native to Japan at all but was, as with so much of their garden flora and culture, imported from China.

The acquisition of these three Oriental species and their subsequent crossing with the smaller European species of *C. viticella* and *C. integrifolia*, gave rise to the modern large-flowered hybrids. The toast of the day in the 1900s, the large-flowered hybrids still make up the bulk of commercial production.

One of the original Oriental species involved in the breeding of large-flowered hybrids, C. patens *(right) is still found growing wild in parts of China and Japan, where it was grown and hybridized in gardens for centuries before reaching Europe in the 1830s. Wild populations vary in colour from deep blue to white, which may be due to their being pollinated by garden hybrids.*

explosion and demise
1860–1920

In the second half of the nineteenth century, nurserymen and gardeners in Britain, France, Belgium and Germany began a frenzy of cross-breeding. Hundreds upon hundreds of new hybrids were created and, though a great number have been lost to cultivation, half the standard clematis varieties offered for sale today can be traced to this extraordinary period in clematis history.

A number of these early hybrids were named after the patrons of nursery gardens, such as 'Lady Betty Balfour', 'Comtesse de Bouchaud' and 'Lord Nevill'. Many nurseries survived through the patronage of the aristocracy, who both sponsored plant collecting and grew the new plants in their gardens. Nurserymen played the key role. One of the best-known clematis hybrids and still one of the most popular is the late large-flowered violet-purple 'Jackmanii'. This was raised in 1858 by Messrs George Jackman & Sons of Woking in Surrey, England. By 1877, Jackman and Moore had published a book listing over 250 clematis cultivars, and by the end of the century there were a further 250.

Other notable breeders in England at this time included Charles Noble of Sunningdale, Surrey, who raised the pure white 'Miss Bateman' (1863), the elegant blue 'Mrs Cholmondeley' (1873) and the purple 'The President' (1876). Messrs Cripps & Sons raised the late-flowering reddish purple 'Gipsy Queen' (1877) and 'Victoria' (1870). In Scotland, Isaac Anderson Henry of Edinburgh was thrilled by his 'Lawsoniana' with flowers up to 24cm across. This clearly was a time when big was beautiful. All these early hybrids were restricted in colour to the whites, mauves and purples of the four parent species: *C. patens*, *C. lanuginosa*, *C. florida* and the European *C. viticella*.

In the 1880s, however, two events occurred which had a great bearing on the future of clematis hybridization. One was responsible for an exciting new revolution, while the other led to utter turmoil.

THE CONTRIBUTION OF *C. TEXENSIS*

In 1868 the startling red clematis *C. texensis*, known then by the name of *C. coccinea* (meaning scarlet), was introduced to Europe from Texas. Although the flower was only small, its scarlet bells revolutionized the shape and colouring of the new hybrids that would appear in their hundreds during the late nineteenth century, introducing pink and red colouring for the first time.

In 1890 the Jackmans successfully crossed *C. texensis* with one of Cripps' large-flowered hybrids, 'Star of India', to produce semi-herbaceous climbers with distinct upright, tulip-shaped flowers. Jackman called this highly refined handful

'Lady Northcliffe' (below) is a cross between 'Beauty of Worcester' and 'Otto Fröbel', introduced by Arthur Jackman and given an Award of Merit in 1906. Named after a patron of the famous Jackmans nursery, it is one of the truly great clematis for gardens. The Wedgwood-blue to deep violet-blue sepals, 10–18cm across, fade to lavender-blue. It is a compact grower, which does best in some shade.

*'Gravetye Beauty' (above) was named to
celebrate the famous gardens of William
Robinson, where he had nurtured so many of the
hybrids given to him by Francisque Morel. This
hybrid is the most renowned, with its narrow
cherry- to ruby-red sepals which, when first open,
take on the form of a tulip but later flatten out
like a star. C. texensis was one of the parents
and it is best placed in full sun. It grows to a
height of 1–2.5m and should be hard pruned;
it is a little prone to mildew.*

his Wokingensis Hybrids; the first two were 'Duchess of Albany', pink, and 'Sir
Trevor Lawrence', rich purple-red. Now grouped under the banner of 'texensis',
they are generally considered the aristocrats of the clematis family. A hundred
years later, breeders are still trying to reproduce these crosses and to create new
hybrids from similar crosses to supersede them – so far with only limited success.

CLEMATIS WILT

Around this time, disaster struck in the form of a disease specific to clematis.
Clematis wilt, possibly occurring as a result of over-breeding, led to the creation
of weak and fragile hybrids, with devastating effect. The symptoms are of a plant
mysteriously collapsing as if from drought. Only a little more is known about this
disease now than back in the late 1800s, but it was rife enough to put many
nurseries out of business and is most certainly the reason why relatively few of
those first 500 hybrids survived.

In France, the nurseryman Francisque Morel, of Lyon, persevered in
breeding a race of *C. viticella* and *C. texensis* hybrids, resulting in some of the best
and most wilt-resistant garden plants available today. They include such well-
known names as 'Perle d'Azur' (1885), 'Royal Velours' (1890s), 'Ville de Lyon'
(1899) and 'Madame Julia Correvon' (1900). Another French nurseryman, Victor
Lemoine of Nancy, in 1883 produced the lively red 'Kermesina' and the white-

and purple-veined 'Venosa Violacea'. Morel soon began collaborating with William Robinson, the most famous – and often controversial – English gardener of his time who had created a garden at Gravetye Manor in Surrey. William Robinson received Morel's 'cast-offs' and, together with his head gardener Ernest Markham, went on to produce a few more of his own.

LATER SPECIES

By 1900, the picture was almost complete. All the important clematis species had been introduced and were growing in gardens, though little more was done with hybridizing them until the 1950s. The two most frequently encountered species of the atragene group, *C. alpina* (from Europe) and *C. macropetala* (from China), both flowering in spring with small, bell-like flowers, had been available since 1768 and 1829 respectively. These now count among the toughest of all clematis and the easiest to grow.

Lady Amherst (immortalized by a beautiful Chinese pheasant that bears her name) had in 1831 introduced from China the glorious *C. montana*, the white-flowered tree-climbing vine which carries a delicate clove scent. By 1900 the pink-flowered form had been discovered by the prolific plant hunter, Ernest Henry Wilson, who went on to introduce the later-flowering *C. montana* var. *wilsonii* (1907) and *C. potaninii* (1911).

The finest evergreen species, *C. armandii*, with its thick leathery leaves and panicles of sweetly scented, early spring flowers, was introduced in 1900 and named in honour of Père Armand David, the French missionary and plant collector. Another scented species with small, soft yellow flowers, *C. rehderiana*, was named after a German botanist and introduced to France in 1898.

A quite distinct kind of clematis is known collectively as the 'orientalis' type; it has mostly yellow rounded or open bells, followed by the fluffiest seedheads of the genus. A species from the province of Tangut, in Tibet, called *C. tangutica* was found in 1898. The form that would become known as the orange peel clematis, due to its thick, rounded sepals, was found in 1937 and first named *C. orientalis* but is now more correctly known as *C. tibetana* subsp. *vernayi*. An improved form was collected by Ludlow, Sherriff and Elliott in 1947.

By the beginning of the twentieth century William Robinson was publishing garden books and magazines in which he often urged the use of clematis in the garden, not simply by growing them up walls and treillage but more naturalistically through trees and shrubs, a system he liked to refer to as 'drapery'. But Robinson's enthusiasm was tempered by the decline of the large-flowered clematis due to wilt, and by the outbreak of the First World War, which was responsible for the demise of many nurseries across Europe. No recovery would really be felt until after the Second World War.

'Rooguchi' is a relatively new hybrid, raised in Japan by Mr K. Ozawa in 1988, from a cross between C. integrifolia *and the much rarer species* C. reticulata *from the USA. This nodding flower in an unusually dark shade has a satiny sheen and is bell-shaped. It lacks the usual*

revival and new enthusiasm
1950 to the present day

After the debilitation caused by wilt and the decline of hybridizing at the start of the twentieth century, clematis badly needed to be given a better name, but it was not until the 1950s that a new generation of nurserymen embarked on a re-launch.

With the increased enthusiasm for gardening following the Second World War, coupled with the trend towards smaller and smaller gardens, came a renewed appreciation of clematis. A clematis could slip neatly into the narrower confines of increasingly restricted-size gardens, both in town and country. This climber also became the perfect cottage gardener's plant, fitting the archetypal image of a little house with a trellised porch draped in clematis and roses, peering out over casual plantings of herbs and flowers. Although this new era included a renewed interest in the large-flowered hybrids, it was the many new hybrids being raised from less susceptible, wilt-free species, such as *C. viticella* and *C. integrifolia*, that would truly come of age.

twisting sepals of many C. integrifolia *hybrids and the sepals remain more or less fused, except near the opening where they flare elegantly. These latter characteristics and its colour are inherited from* C. reticulata. *'Rooguchi' grows to a height of 2m, needing the support of other plants.*

THE GLOBALIZATION OF CLEMATIS

The latter half of the twentieth century saw a boom in clematis hybrids, unmatched since those heady days a hundred years before. There are now over a thousand hybrids available worldwide and, although many are very similar to one another, there have been notable breakthroughs by inspired breeders the world over, including Estonia, Japan, Canada, the USA, New Zealand, Poland, Sweden and the Ukraine. Many new varieties were given their first outing at a flower show, where the pot-grown, large-flowered clematis displayed themselves proudly, perhaps sensing all the attention and admiration. The International Clematis Society was founded in 1984 and whereas in the 1960s only one or two books were available on the subject of clematis, there are now several hundred, reflecting the progressive, well-deserved interest in the genus.

During the 1960s and 1970s there was a hive of activity in England, with well-known breeders raising and introducing new hybrids from the USA, Sweden and Poland, and exhibiting them at major flower shows. Walter Pennell of Lincolnshire was part of that revival, raising the ever-popular velvety double 'Vyvyan Pennell', the vividly striped 'Mrs N. Thompson' and one of the most reliable blues in 'H. F. Young'. Jim Fisk in Norfolk introduced the peerless dark red 'Niobe', from Poland, and raised the exquisite wavy white 'Gillian Blades'.

Meanwhile in Europe, Girault of Orléans, France, grew the sumptuous red-toned 'Voluceau' and 'Rouge Cardinal'. And the experiments of Brother Stefan, a Polish Jesuit monk, added deeper and more velvety colour and textures to the large-flowered hybrids, with varieties such as 'Westerplatte', 'Kardynal Wyszynski' and 'Warszawska Nike'. He also produced the indispensable 'Polish Spirit', 'General Sikorski' and Blue Angel.

From the late 1960s to the early 1980s, John Treasure of Shropshire, and later his manager Raymond Evison, stirred up excitement every spring with their fabulous displays at the Chelsea Flower Show in London. Treasure, who raised the three superb varieties 'Pagoda', 'Fireworks' and 'Royalty', initially set up his nursery in a quasi-partnership with the well-known garden writer Christopher Lloyd of Great Dixter. Raymond Evison has since become one of the great champions of clematis, spreading the message worldwide from the island of Guernsey in the Channel Islands, where he has built up his nursery into a veritable clematis empire. He inaugurated the International Clematis Society and has raised and introduced countless new varieties, mostly large-flowered hybrids, such as the double white Arctic Queen, frilly pink Josephine, a green-centred form of *C. florida* called Pistachio and 'Guernsey Cream'.

SMALL-FLOWERED HYBRIDS

The real interest of the last two or three decades lay in the small-flowered hybrids. Gardeners have become increasingly discerning and sophisticated and now seek out less blowsy and less blatant plants. Fortunately, these refined new hybrids often tend to be a good deal easier to grow.

Perhaps the most successful and elusive of the latter-day breeders is Barry Fretwell of Peveril Clematis Nursery in Devon, England. He raised the superb pink texensis-type 'Princess Diana' as well as the pendulous

The Oriental species C. fusca is a curious creature with brown hairy flowers. It is very variable in its wild state: C. fusca var. violacea, with its thick, violet sepals (below), is one of its forms. The violet forms have been crossed with C. integrifolia to produce 'Fascination' and 'Michelle', new hybrids with violet-purple bell-shaped flowers and attractive seedheads.

'Warszawska Nike' (above) was raised in Poland in 1966 by Brother Stefan Franczak, a Jesuit priest, to commemorate the freedom fighters of Warsaw in the Second World War. Brother Stefan rarely acknowledges the parentage of his hybrids, of which there are many. Growing to 3m, this form can be light or hard pruned.

C. × *diversifolia* 'Heather Herschell' and 'Arabella', a non-stop herbaceous plant which has proved ideal for training on obelisks in pots. His 'Lord Herschell', a dark purple tulip-shaped flower on dwarf *C. integrifolia* growth, deserves to come out of the shadows of its relative obscurity.

On a global level, certain hybridizers have proved just how hardy clematis can be. In Manitoba, Canada, Frank Skinner has raised 'Pamela', 'Blue Bird' and *C.* × *diversifolia* 'Blue Boy', while in the USA, near to New York, Arthur Steffen has produced the compact 'The First Lady' and the purple 'Perrin's Pride', and has introduced 'Betty Corning', a *C. crispa* hybrid with unusual pale blue bells on light, airy growth. The late Magnus Johnson raised a host of new bone-hardy atragenes in Helsingborg, Sweden, while Uno Kivistik of Estonia was creating a range of tough hybrids of the viticella and Jackmanii types, like the dark purple 'Viola' and 'Romantika'. Professor Beskaravainaja, from the Ukraine, raised the tall herbaceous pink 'Alionushka' and 'Paul Farges', a rampant small-flowered white hybrid of *C. potaninii*.

At the more tender extreme, a new race of clematis, known as the New Zealanders, have been raised by, among others, Alister Keay and Joe Cartman. Mostly derived from three native species, *C. paniculata*, *C. forsteri* and *C. marmoraria*, these smaller plants are evergreen, white- or green-flowered and some are deliciously scented. Sadly, most are suitable only for gardens with a milder climate or for greenhouses. Alister Keay has also introduced some hardy late hybrids, the easy and long-flowering blue 'Prince Charles' and one of the darkest of all viticellas, 'Black Prince'.

THE WAY FORWARD

From Japan we have seen the introduction of brilliant new large-flowered clematis like 'Asao', Pink Champagne, 'Hakuookan', Wada's Primrose and the nearest to pure blue in 'Fuji-musume'. But we should also expect a new race of *C. florida* hybrids to enter our nursery lists soon, some of which are crosses with *C. integrifolia*, like 'Aphrodite', 'Rising Star' and 'Fukuzono' – all stars of the future. The same may be true of hybrids between such species such as *C. viticella* and *C. integrifolia*, where it all began in the 1830s.

Other, rarer species are being experimented upon, such as the strange purple- and brown-flowered *C. fusca* (introduced in 1840), and other relatives of *C. texensis*, such as *C. viorna*, the vase vine of the USA, and *C. pitcheri*. These new hybrids tend to be smaller plants, suitable for city gardens and container culture. The results are plants like 'Kaiu', a vigorous plant with small white thick-sepalled bells, or more mysterious plants with dark colours and unusual shapes like 'Fascination', Petit Faucon and 'Rooguchi' (see page 14).

habitats and habits

Nearly 300 species of clematis are now known to botanists, although only 20-30 species are usually grown by gardeners. Of these 300, around 17 species are native to Europe, 108 to China, 11 to Russia, 35 to North America and five to New Zealand, while possibly over a hundred come from subtropical or tropical countries, like India and Java. Knowing how a plant grows in its native habitat can give us many clues about how to use it in a garden.

HARDINESS

The majority of clematis are surprisingly hardy. Those featured in this book are all hardy in the temperate world, though one or two, especially the evergreens, may need protection in colder districts. Most large-flowered hybrids can live in extreme cold and are quite happy in fairly damp, but not waterlogged, situations. A testament to how tough many of these climbers can be is the number of enthusiastic clematis growers living in cool-climate countries like Sweden, Canada, the Baltic States, Poland and the Ukraine. But it would be folly to try growing more delicate clematis like the evergreens in these northerly countries.

Generally speaking, clematis dislike heat and will not thrive in tropical conditions; exceptions include species like *C. flammula* and *C. cirrhosa* which come from southern Europe and the Mediterranean. Two species closely related to *C. flammula* – *C. recta* and *C. terniflora* – also hail from drier parts of the world. All three have clouds of small white flowers in late summer. Native to Japan and China, *C. terniflora* has become naturalized in many parts of the east coast of the USA, where it is known, incorrectly, as *C. paniculata*.

Like many evergreen clematis, the New Zealand species, such as the true *C. paniculata* and *C. forsteri*, prefer a dry winter and sufficient moisture during the growing season. This is the reverse of conditions found in many European or North American gardens, where it is often wet in winter and dry in summer. Most of this group are only hardy down to -8°C and should thrive in an unheated greenhouse. At the other extreme, the atragenes are mountaineers and used to both cold and wind. They tend to have finer foliage, tighter growth and small flowers.

HABITATS

In his book on clematis species, Christopher Grey-Wilson vividly describes their haunts as rocky places and cliffs, river banks and rocks, dry mountainsides, the edge of woodlands and mountain scrub. He quotes Reginald Farrer on seeing a form of *C. tangutica* in China in 1921, 'unfurling a coil almost as long as its name over the river shingles of all the streams above Jo-ni, ascending to about 10,000ft on

C. patens *grows wild in the mountains of Iwate prefecture in Northern Honshu, Japan. Here it makes its home in open clearings in the forest, alongside other opportunist vines that clamber among viburnums, cherries and spiraeas.* C. patens *is the dominant parent of all the early large-flowered hybrids.*

the fringes of the alpine coppice'. Ernest Wilson, the English plant hunter, writing of a trip to China in 1903, describes a scene near the summit of a mountain 3,000m high: 'A slightly undulating plateau, many acres in extent, with thickets of tall Rhododendrons festooned with *Clematis montana* var. *wilsonii*, and clumps of Silver Fir, the offspring of giants which once clothed this magnificent mountain.'

In the wild clematis can be seen scrambling and sprawling over rocks and bushes in scrubby areas, near streams or occasionally in open grassland. Some clematis, despite having the ability to climb, grow to form shrubby mounds in rocky grassland. Beneath the rocks their roots can often find a rare patch of moisture and they can eke out an existence, sequestered away from the sun and competition from other plants. In imitation of this, I have grown *C. flammula*, *C. alpina*, *C. montana* and *C. orientalis* types alone in gravelled areas of the garden, where moisture is retained beneath matting and mulches. Here they seem to grow better than in dense mixed plantings of shrubs and perennials, enjoying the reflected light and heat from the gravel. Large-flowered hybrids would tend to burn up in the same conditions, preferring a cooler setting.

C. patens, the parent of most early large-flowered hybrids, grows as an opportunist in cleared woodlands in its native Japan. In northern Honshu, at an altitude of 260m above sea-level, I saw a plant covering a good 4m^2 of ground and another reaching 2–3m up into neighbouring shrubs such as berberis and small cherries. As soon as the forest closes in, *C. patens* starts to lose out, but it will clamber up shrubs that edge out into the clearings, creating a dense carpet. The scene, as is so often is the case with open glades where trees fall or loose rocks are shifting, is rather like a garden – a space of suspense and movement. The clematis, a marginal opportunist, takes perfect advantage of this and exploiting clematis in such a way in the garden can make for truly dynamic plantings.

THE CLIMBING HABIT

Unlike sweet peas, clematis do not possess tendrils, nor do their stems wind around other plants, like a wisteria. Instead their leaf stalks (petioles) twist round any support they can find, especially small twigs, wires, string or light trelliswork. The few species of herbaceous clematis have no ability to climb, in winter dying down to their crowns at ground level. *C. integrifolia* and *C. recta* often become leggy and floppy in the garden, unused to soft, fertile conditions. In their native habitat they would be starved a little of both food and water, making them grow shorter and more erect. Some hybrids between herbaceous types and climbing species inherit the inability to climb with a capacity to grow up to 2m tall. This is an unnatural state for a clematis, so gardeners have to invent ways to support them. They will need to grow through a web of wires or the matrix of a well-branched shrub, such as a shrub rose or a large hydrangea.

classification guide

Clematis belong to the same plant family as the buttercup (*Ranunculus*), in the order known as the Ranunculaceae. Other members of this family include *Helleborus, Aquilegia, Anemone, Pulsatilla, Thalictrum* and *Caltha*, to which some of the clematis species bear a striking resemblance. The shape of the flower of *Clematis macropetala*, for example, can be favourably compared to an aquilegia, *C. cirrhosa* to a hellebore, *C. montana* to an anemone, and *C. vitalba* to goat's rue (*Thalictrum*). The main difference is that the flowers of clematis are not in fact made up of petals, which are generally absent, but sepals. In most plants sepals form the casing that protects the flower buds as they open, but in clematis these have become so highly developed and coloured that they are, in effect, the flower.

The simplest way to break down this extremely diverse genus is to subdivide it into two culturally distinct (though botanically incorrect) groups: the early-flowering species and their hybrids, cultivars and variants, and the late-flowering species and their hybrids, cultivars and variants. This is indeed a major over-simplification – and not just as far as the botanist is concerned. It requires a clear distinction between what constitutes early flowering and what is late flowering: early-flowering clematis are those that flower on shoots breaking from wood made during the previous season, while the late-flowering kinds flower on new wood or growth made during the current growing season. Once we understand this distinction clearly, it will also help to clarify the widely divergent pruning needs of different clematis (see pages 138–41).

A GARDENER'S CLASSIFICATION

There are many complicated botanical classifications for clematis, which are of interest mainly to the specialist, but gardeners and nurserymen generally accept the following broader classification and this is the one followed in the portrait gallery (Choosing Clematis, pages 62–131).

1. EARLY-FLOWERING SPECIES AND HYBRIDS (Pruning Group One)

A. EVERGREEN CLEMATIS This group includes the winter-flowering *C. cirrhosa*, the New Zealanders *C. paniculata* and *C. marmoraria*, the Oriental *C. armandii* and a few other species that flower before early spring. Though they generally need little or no pruning, if they become ungainly this group can be hard pruned immediately after flowering, as they still have all year to generate new wood. The evergreens tend to be the least hardy of all clematis.

B. THE ATRAGENES The spring-flowering atragenes are among the hardiest of all clematis. This distinct group is dominated in gardens by two species: *C. alpina* is native to the alpine regions of Europe, while *C. macropetala* takes over further east, in China and in the Himalayas.

C. alpina

C. spooneri

C. THE MONTANAS *C. montana* is a familiar garden plant of late spring, partly because it grows tall and is therefore clearly visible, climbing high into trees and over fences. It has been hybridized with *C. chrysocoma* and most forms in this group are creamy white or shades of pale pink through to deep mauve-pink. Many, but not all, are fragrant, smelling a bit like vanilla or cloves.

2. LARGE-FLOWERED HYBRIDS

A. EARLY FLOWERING (Pruning Group Two)

This group of early summer flowering forms comprises what most gardeners would recognize as clematis. The single forms have large, flattened flowers with five to eight sepals, 10–23cm across, and stamens that vary from cream to reddish purple. The large-flowered hybrids that bloom before midsummer are all products of the three species *C. patens, C. florida* and *C. lanuginosa*, rarely seen outside specialist collections. Of their numerous hybrids, a minority are double and semi-double. All these hybrids come in an astonishing array of colours, except yellow or orange, while others are distinctively striped.

C. 'Elsa Spath'

B. LATE FLOWERING (Pruning Group Three)

Most of these are similar to the early-flowering hybrids, but are rarely double or striped; they flower in mid- to late summer. They are sometimes known as the Jackmanii group, after its most famous member, *C.* 'Jackmanii'. They carry *C. viticella* blood, which gives them their late-flowering characteristic. Some straddle this and the viticella group (see below), but their treatment and cultivation are identical.

3. LATE-FLOWERING SPECIES AND SMALL-FLOWERED HYBRIDS
(Pruning Group Three)

A. THE VITICELLAS

This group mostly comprises the forms closest to *C. viticella* itself, a vigorous, fine-leaved climber with smaller flowers and leaves than the Jackmanii group. The viticellas are hardy, disease-resistant and trouble-free, making them one of the most versatile of clematis for mixed and more naturalistic plantings.

B. THE TEXENSIS GROUP

The main characteristic of this aristocratic group is the form of the flower, which in the majority of cases is urn-shaped. Most species come from the USA, including *C. texensis*, the species used in the majority of today's hybrids. Many texensis hybrids have a large-flowered clematis as a parent, producing a unique and distinctive tulip-shaped flower. Some modern breeders have been raising plants from other species within the texensis group like *C. fusca, C. pitcheri* and *C. viorna*.

C. HERBACEOUS SPECIES AND HYBRIDS

These diverse clematis are simply cut back each year as they naturally die down to ground level. Of all species, *C. heracleifolia* is least like a clematis, with its vine-shaped leaves and whorls of blue flowers on upright stems. *C. integrifolia*, by contrast, is a small floppy plant growing to only 1m, with twisted sepals. One of the oldest known species of clematis, *C. integrifolia* may belong to the texensis group, but due to its distinctly herbaceous habit tends to be grouped with other herbaceous clematis.

D. THE ORIENTALIS GROUP

This group includes the profuse tangutica types with their fountains of growth and yellow lanterns, made up of sepals as thick as orange peel, followed by handsome silvery seedheads.

C. Golden Tiara

E. OTHER LATE-FLOWERING SPECIES

Included here are old man's beard (*C. vitalba*) as well as such elegant plants as *C. rehderiana* and *C. potaninii*.

clematis in the
garden

Clematis is a vast and versatile genus, with plants of all heights and eye-catching flowers in a wide range of sizes, shapes and colours. They can be trained to scale walls and fences or may simply be allowed to cascade down them. Clematis are at their best twining through trees and shrubs and may be planted in beds and borders to grow through perennials or just trail along the ground. Many of the smaller varieties can be grown successfully in containers and window boxes. In both large and small gardens there are infinite possibilities for clematis and, once you have mastered their culture, you will be tempted to experiment with growing them in all sorts of situations. It will simply be a matter of choosing the right clematis for the season and matching their height, habit and colour to suit your taste and situation.

'Blue Dancer' (left) is a form of C. macropetala *with an accentuated droop to its pendulous flowers.* C. montana *var.* rubens *'Odorata' flowers simultaneously on another wall.*

selecting clematis

A good garden centre or nursery should offer well over a hundred excellent varieties of clematis and at least the same number again are available from more specialist nurseries. Some of the best varieties, now tried and tested for over 150 years, remain among the finest of all garden plants. No garden is too small or too large, too formal or too wild to provide a home for 'the queen of climbers'.

SMALL GARDENS

Clematis are ideal for small spaces, because their preferred dimension is upwards. Even the smallest town garden could accommodate at least ten clematis, as well as other plants like roses and smaller shrubs. Grown in pots on the patio, twining through a shrub rose, covering a fence or archway, or simply climbing a house wall, another clematis can always be fitted in, even if your garden appears to be full.

I have visited a garden in Japan, measuring 70m by 10m, in which an amateur grower has established over 2,000 clematis – as well as several camellias, irises and daylilies. An English grower, whose garden of only 15m by 10m includes a lawn, some shrubs and a terrace, has over 200 varieties. These examples may carry enthusiasm to excess, but they illustrate what is possible if you are smitten by clematis! A garden stuffed with clematis, however, is far less attractive than one in which a well-chosen few are carefully placed and grown with other plants.

In a small garden you will seek even greater value from your plants and will want as long a season as possible (see Clematis for all seasons, page 26). A restricted plot does not mean that the clematis you choose must be small. Town houses are often tall enough to take a *C. montana* or *C. orientalis*, both of which can reach to 8m. Even these species, pruned strategically, can be kept within more manageable bounds. For small plots, the real stars are likely to be found among the atragenes and large-flowered hybrids. Although some reach 4–5m unchecked, others grow to only 1.5m, among them compact dual-season varieties like 'Niobe'.

Bear in mind that not all clematis are attractive all-rounders when out of flower. Most early large-flowered hybrids, though occasionally bearing impressive balls of seeds, can be a sorry set of brown foliage and mouldy flowerheads by late summer. It might be more satisfying to grow such clematis through other plants, such as viburnums, ceanothus or roses, where much of the unsightly mess can be camouflaged under their canopies (see Through shrubs and trees, page 44).

If your garden is of a medium size, say 50m by 25m, there will be countless opportunities for growing clematis. Look to those dully dressed shrubs in late summer, or old, misshapen conifers, or that climbing rose that is bare for half its height – a clematis will help to enliven them all.

Like a miniature large-flowered hybrid on herbaceous growth, 'Arabella' is a real star for small gardens, with a compact, malleable habit and a long flowering season. Growing 1–2m tall, it is easily tucked into a mixed border at the base of roses or shrubs, where some growth flops forward and some reaches into the shrub's branches.

Where space permits, two or more clematis can be grown on a frame or obelisk in a border. Choose those that flower simultaneously for maximum impact. Here, 'Hagley Hybrid' is partnered with 'Jackmanii Superba', both flowering in midsummer. 'Hagley Hybrid' is is a profuse and reliable performer, tinged with mauve. The clematis, sweet pea and perennials like anthemis will all be cut back in winter.

LARGER GARDENS

Here the choice is much greater, with many lovely clematis growing above 5m. Some can be trained into trees, along fences, over outbuildings or even be allowed to form mounds of ground-cover. Lessons about planting clematis in a large country garden can be gained from seeing the wild traveller's joy (*C. vitalba*) in the landscape, where it may tangle among the lower branches of oaks or smother a hazel. This is not the ideal garden plant, but other vigorous clematis, like 'Bill MacKenzie' or *C. tangutica*, are garden-worthy forms which look wonderful from the moment their first flowers open in early summer until the new year. Their yellow lantern-like flowers continue into late summer and eventually turn to silvery white seedheads. This metamorphosis from a mass of blooms to a mound of shining silver is a joy to watch and a reason to include such clematis in a garden.

WILD AND FORMAL GARDENS

Clematis do not lend themselves well to formal gardens, especially if you want strict symmetry. It would be hard to tame a clematis to behave with flawless discipline. It is in their nature to be wayward and to wander off into places you never intended – and therein lies their beauty. At times they may simply be perverse, their leaves or whole shoots shrivelling to a crisp brown – not dying, but retiring from the fray – and this, in the middle of summer, would be sure to upset a formal gardener. A better solution would be to train a rose on an obelisk and allow a clematis such as 'Blue Boy' to wind its way through the rose.

In the wilder parts of a large garden many clematis, like the montanas or the orientalis group, can be left to romp around unattended, unpruned and unfed. These larger-growing clematis behave like rambler roses: if you start them off well, you can leave them to it. Wait for that surprise thread of growth, teasing its way to the light to drop a bloom-laden strand before you, and enjoy the unpredictability.

clematis for all seasons

One of the great merits of clematis, apart from their variety of shape, size and colour, is their range of flowering times. Unlike roses or azaleas, or indeed most plants that are confined to a single season, there can be a species of clematis in flower almost every month of the year. In a mild temperate garden, if you were to choose even five clematis, you could plan to have at least one in flower from early spring through to winter. In colder climates this may be limited to the period from late spring to autumn, but the lack of flowers in winter can be made up for by choosing varieties that bear attractive seedheads.

Defining the seasons precisely can be tricky, as this greatly depends on location. In extremely cold climates the summers are squeezed into a couple of months, a period that elsewhere is called mid- to late summer. Hotter and milder climates might well force so-called late-summer varieties to complete their show much earlier. There may also be a variance in flowering time according to how much pruning is done (see pages 138–41) and on degrees of sun or shade, with plants grown in shade flowering later than those in full sun.

To plan a full year of clematis, choose about ten varieties, selecting at least one from each of the different groups, such as an evergreen, an atragene, a montana, two or three early- and late-season large-flowered hybrids, a viticella or texensis, a late species like *C. rehderiana* and a good seed-bearer like the orientalis type 'Bill MacKenzie'. If you do not have space for the last two or a montana, grow an extra atragene, like *C. macropetala* for its seedheads, and a few of the herbaceous integrifolias.

WINTER

C. cirrhosa is the only winter-flowering clematis with any pretence to hardiness. Native to the Mediterranean rim and its islands, its hardiness is rather variable, and it is unsuitable for very cold gardens. The hardiest is the fern-leaved form, *C. cirrhosa* var. *balearica*, which carries its small cream bells from early winter onwards. Like its winter-flowering relative the hellebore, its flower buds are remarkably frost resistant, remaining undamaged by frosts of -6°C and possibly colder.

By far the best seedheads are carried from late summer through winter by members of the orientalis group, and the star of these is *C. tangutica*, especially its form 'Lambton Park', which has not only bigger flowers than the type but correspondingly larger fluffy seedheads. Plant it next to shrubs with evergreen foliage or bright winter stems, like *Cornus alba* 'Sibirica', in order to accentuate its qualities and preferably in a position where the early-morning or late-evening sun will highlight the seedheads.

SEASONAL STARS (opposite)

1 Winter *The flowering period of C. cirrhosa is influenced by the harshness of the winter. A mild late autumn and winter brings on an early flowering that is mostly over by the new year, while a harder winter delays flowering, which then carries on into early spring. This form, var. balearica, from the Mediterranean Balearic Islands is one of the hardiest, with attractively lobed and fern-like leaves and plentiful but marginally smaller creamy white flowers, dotted inside with maroon.*

2 Spring *The atragenes are the first of the really hardy spring-flowering clematis. 'Ballet Skirt' was raised in 1981 by Stanley Zubrowski in Saskatchewan, Canada, a testimony to its hardiness. Its larger, paler pink mother plant is 'Rosy O'Grady', also raised in Canada.*

3 Early summer *'Richard Pennell' is a large-flowered hybrid with a very handsome 'full' flower, its overlapping rich purple-blue sepals neatly surrounding a boss of golden-yellow anthers. The rich colour fades to a paler blue, especially if displayed in full sun. It was raised by Pennells of Lincoln in 1962, as a cross between 'Vyvyan Pennell' and 'Daniel Deronda'.*

4 Late summer *'Polish Spirit' is a rich dark purple variety whose small flowers, 5–10cm across, show a close affinity with the viticellas. Flowering in late summer, it can look startling among the bright young shoots of golden conifers or the autumn berries of evergreens, here a cotoneaster and a rowan. Raised in Poland by Brother Franczak, 1984.*

SPRING

Gardeners who fall in love with the evergreen New Zealand species, flowering in early spring, may have to be content to keep them in a cold greenhouse as they are hardy only down to around -10°C. Under glass, they may even start flowering in late winter. One of the finest of this group is a new hybrid called 'Avalanche', with pure white flowers showing well against finely cut, rich green foliage. Some in this group have green flowers, like *C. forsteri*, which also carries a heavenly scent.

C. armandii, another scented evergreen but a stronger-growing species, flowers in mid-spring and is reasonably hardy. Because its flower buds and leathery foliage are somewhat prone to damage from cold winds, it is best planted in a sheltered position, ideally in a corner spot protected by two walls.

Mid-spring is also the season for the atragenes, some of the loveliest but simplest of clematis. Characterized by their small, pendulous flowers set amid finely cut, soft green foliage, these are also the toughest of all clematis and the most trouble-free. The group is dominated in gardens by *C. alpina*, with four simple sepals, and *C. macropetala* with its double ruffled flower. Both species are blue in their natural state but have given rise to many new varieties in white and pink, through to deep purple. *C. macropetala* is one of the most beautiful of all species clematis and has barely been improved on by breeders. Its silver seedheads look good well into late summer but start to become a bit mangy by winter.

In late spring, as the danger of frosts subsides, *C. montana* pushes out its tender growth and small round flower buds. One or two degrees of frost too many and the whole display can be lost. This hugely popular clematis is fast becoming a familiar celebrant of spring, climbing up fences, houses and trees. *C. montana* var. *wilsonii*, with white flowers, blooms a week or two later than the species and most of its forms.

LARGE-FLOWERED HYBRIDS

These hybrids are of such mixed parentage that they vary hugely in their time of flowering. The early-flowering kinds may produce another flush or two later in the season, while the later Jackmanii types flower once only, from mid- to late summer. One of the earliest of the first group to flower is 'Guernsey Cream', opening two to three weeks ahead of the majority which start in late spring and run on into the rose season. Their buds start swelling in late winter and early spring, producing long shoots complete with flower buds pushing out for up to 15cm, at a time when frosts may still be knocking the blooms off magnolias and camellias. These clematis shoots are rarely damaged but any early over-exposure to prolonged cold may discolour the flowers when they open, rendering them colourless and green.

The montanas (above) sometimes overlap or bridge the seasons between the atragenes and the early large-flowered hybrids. Opening at the end of spring, their young growth and flower buds, just like those of wisteria, are still vulnerable to late frosts. Wisteria is one of the few climbers that combine well in colour and vigour with C. montana, *and both are fragrant. The scent of this clematis varies from cloves to vanilla. Late frosts barely affect other spring-flowering clematis.*

SUMMER

The mid-season large-flowered hybrids, blooming in early summer, belong to a group that shows intermediate characteristics between the early and late hybrids. If you wish to grow only large-flowered hybrids, their season can be extended by choosing a few from this group, to bridge the flowering times of the other two. 'Marie Boisselot', 'Ramona' and 'W. E. Gladstone' all flower significantly later than the main flush of the earlier group.

As the first flush of roses fades, and the irises and peonies are over, the high-summer garden of buddlejas and hydrangeas begins. This is when the late-flowering hybrids or Jackmanii group of clematis start to bloom, together with various small-flowered species and their hybrids. All clematis mentioned so far have bloomed from buds formed in the previous summer, in the axils of mature shoots. There is a point in the midsummer season when clematis start to flower on entirely new shoots that have pushed out since the beginning of the year. 'Madame Julia Correvon' and 'M. Koster' are the first of these.

The late-summer season is one that gardeners often neglect, but you could bring your garden to life with a selection of integrifolias, viticellas, texensis, orientalis, heracleifolias and late species like *C. rehderiana* and *C. terniflora*, some continuing into early autumn. It is hard to say which will be the first to flower, because the mixed parentage of many clematis makes it unpredictable, but *C. potaninii*, a species from China with small white flowers, blooms quite early in summer, while 'Paul Farges', its hybrid with *C. vitalba*, and 'Anita', a hybrid between *C. potaninii* and *C. tangutica*, flower much later in the season.

The flowering time of each of the above groups also varies from region to region and from sun to shade. Much depends on the kind of summer too. Where summer arrives almost overnight, everything tends to happen at once and both spring and summer can merge in an explosion of colour. Where summers are dry and very hot, many of the late clematis will flower, brown off and die back; in this case they may be deliberately cut back to bloom again in the cool of early autumn. In the mild, damp climate of temperate and maritime areas, the summer season may be longer and late-flowering clematis might carry on into autumn. Even early large-flowered hybrids, if they are well-fed and deadheaded, will throw up a late flush.

The longest-flowering clematis naturally have great value in the garden. One of the finest clematis ever raised is the pink tulip-shaped texensis hybrid 'Princess Diana'. Not only does it have an extended flowering season, starting in midsummer and lasting for eight weeks or more, but it suffers none of the defects of many texensis types. Other long-flowering clematis include 'Anita', 'Prince Charles' and 'Arabella', all late-season varieties whose flowering is sometimes only brought to a halt by the advent of frost.

The yellow lantern flowers of the orientalis group clematis 'Bill MacKenzie' (below) turn to seed progressively so that by autumn the silvery seedheads smother the entire plant. Originally found in Waterperry Gardens in southern England, in 1968, this clematis is named after a curator of the Chelsea Physic Garden in London.

flower form and colour

With flowers ranging from the exquisitely tiny, only 1cm in diameter and usually carried in profuse clusters, to show-stopping large blooms up to 20cm across, the clematis family is remarkable for its variety and can be a source of deep intrigue too. The first image that springs to mind may well be the large, flat, open flowers of a classic like the pink striped 'Nelly Moser', so simple and obvious in its make-up that it is the kind of flower a child might draw. In reality there are seemingly endless permutations with clematis flowers, all of which hybridizers love to exploit, in the shapes of open and closed bells, lanterns, bugles, vases and tulips.

Although so varied, the different forms within this genus necessarily share certain characteristics in their flower structure. Clematis flowers are basically quite simple and symmetrical, like the other members of the Ranunculaceae order, such as buttercups and anemones. What appear like petals are actually sepals, most commonly four but sometimes as many as eight. The sepals are held tightly together in the bud and forced apart in the flower of most species; they can be fleshy and thick in texture. In some clematis the sepals remain fused at the base.

C. texensis and its close relatives all have a characteristic urn-shaped flower, with an opening like pursed lips, just wide enough to allow small insects inside to pollinate them. Known as the vase vine in its native America, breeders have exploited *C. viorna*'s unusual shape. The crossing of the pendulous vase-shaped species with upward-facing, flat-flowered hybrids has resulted in the upturned tulip shape of 'Duchess of Albany' and 'Sir Trevor Lawrence'. The texensis-group clematis 'Pagoda' is pendulous like its other ancestor, *C. viticella*, but its thicker pale mauve sepals have beautifully up-curving tips, alluded to in a name that evokes the roofs of Oriental architecture. This it inherits from 'Étoile Rose'.

C. rehderiana, a late-flowering species from China, has clusters of cream or pale yellow flowers that hang down like small bells, while above the main flower a stray primrose bract waves like a small flag. *C. integrifolia* carries pendulous flowers with splayed sepals that curl like the skirt of a pirouetting dancer.

A quartered bell, or lantern, shape is common to two groups, the spring-flowering atragenes and the summer-flowering orientalis group. Little has been done to improve this exquisite form and hybrids between these groups and others are rare. Within these groups are many selected forms where the bells flare open like the blades of a propeller, as in 'Helios' and Golden Tiara in the orientalis group and 'Willy' in the atragenes.

The herbaceous *C. heracleifolia* and *C. tubulosa* groups look nothing like a clematis. The bold, vine-shaped foliage resembles that of a Japanese anemone and in late summer the spikes carry two or three whorls of blue bugle-shaped flowers.

'Duchess of Albany' is a texensis group clematis with a unique upturned tulip shape. A deep candy-pink band down the centre of each sepal softens to lilac-pink at the margins. Raised by Arthur Jackman, 1890.

GALAXY OF SHAPES (opposite)

1 The bell or lantern form is common to many orientalis-group clematis, with sepals as thick as orange peel. 'Last Dance' is a Dutch form whose flowers become more orange as they age and are followed by fluffy seedheads.

2 The name 'Pagoda' alludes to the splayed and reflexed sepals, which also twist at the tip. The backs of the flowers have much denser colouring. Raised by John Treasure, 1980.

3 'Nelly Moser' is the most popular of the striped clematis. The flat, open flower looks distinctly modern in style but it was raised before 1897 by Moser et Fils of Versailles, France.

4 The double 'Vyvyan Pennell' has a broad base of two or three layers of rosy lavender sepals that later open more fully. Raised by Walter Pennell in 1959, it is prone to clematis wilt.

5 The natural shape of C. integrifolia sepals is pendulous and twisted, the twisting inherited by many hybrids including 'Tapestry', shown here. These low herbaceous plants reach to only 1m.

6 'Annemieke' is a Dutch hybrid whose flowers flare out like a propeller. Its midsummer flowering is short-lived but profuse, followed by fine seeds.

DOUBLES AND SEMI-DOUBLES

A double flower is one where, by a quirk of nature, some of the stamens transmute into petals or sepals. The style of the doubling depends on the number of stamens that change, a fully double being one where the whole flower fills out in a big frilly mass, while a semi-double simply adds another layer of sepals. Some double clematis are as flouncy as Easter bonnets and sophisticated gardeners tend to scoff at their exhibitionism. Even if some belong more to the catwalk than the garden, they are undeniably fabulous; their popularity in the 1880s is no surprise. Today they are so commonplace that we are in danger of taking them for granted.

    C. macropetala is the only naturally occurring double clematis. It is quite remarkable in the complexity of its flower, where a bush of silvery white and blue staminodes fluffs out. The early large-flowered hybrids have thrown up an array of doubles – some, like 'Duchess of Edinburgh', fully double and others, like 'Jackmanii Rubra', semi-double. *C. montana* has a number of double forms too, such as 'Broughton Star' and 'Marjorie', often quite spiky in appearance.

1 'Moonlight', a large-flowered creamy yellow variety, caused great excitement when it arrived from Sweden, originally called 'Yellow Queen'. A light and frail grower, it is best grown in some shade, otherwise any hint of yellow will bleach out. Raised by Tage Lundell, 1968.

2 C. florida var. flore-pleno is a double form of C. florida, almost certainly grown in Oriental gardens for centuries before its introduction to Europe in 1835. The flowers eventually turn white, especially in full sun, but with a little shade may retain their delicious creamy greenness until they drop. Flecks of purple in the central boss of shorter sepals hint at their metamorphosis from the rich purple stamens of the species.

3 Clear yellow is not found in any clematis except the orientalis group. 'Lambton Park' has some of the largest flowers in the group and of the clearest buttercup-yellow. Its seedheads are a mass of large, long-lasting balls of silver.

4 Although pink forms of C. montana are more common in cultivation, the wild form is most often white. White is the colour most frequently found among tall-growing clematis species, many of them displayed at their best when grown through evergreens.

Clematis colours range from the sharpest yellow through to scarlet, purple, blues, pinks, cream and white. Orange is lacking, but this is perhaps not a significant shortcoming as it is one of the least popular colours in the garden. Colour choice is, of course, very personal but I find that some of the very bright or stripey large-flowered hybrids look out of place in naturalistic plantings. Whites and blues are easy to weave into almost any scheme, while some pinks clash with the harsher yellows and gold. None of the reds found in clematis are too strident for inclusion in a planting scheme; they appear more subdued when combined with purple.

GREEN A colour beloved of flower arrangers and plantsmen, green is found in a few clematis, particularly the New Zealand species. The popularity of this group will be limited by their dislike of cold and wet, though they look good in pots indoors. The old large-flowered double white 'Duchess of Edinburgh' is quite green when it first opens and, if kept in some shade, stays green for a week or two. Also pale green in its first flush, *C. florida* var. *flore-pleno* later loses that tinge, while the white viticella 'Alba Luxurians' retains its green sepal tips for longer.

YELLOW Eye-catching bright yellow is present in a number of the orientalis group, such as 'Bill MacKenzie'. *C. koreana* is mostly yellow, though it produces dark red and bluish forms, too. A creamier yellow characterizes *C. rehderiana*, *C. aethusifolia* and *C. cirrhosa*. A new race of *C. montana* hybrids also has a pretence to yellow in its make-up, one double form being named 'Primrose Star'; in fact it is more cream, fading in sun to pure white. Wada's Primrose and 'Guernsey Cream' are among some of the most beautiful of the large-flowered group.

WHITE White appears in all clematis groups, in every shape and size, double and semi-double. White flowers look good against dark evergreens like yew or holly.

The New Zealand species are either green or white. *C. paniculata* and its offspring 'Avalanche' and 'Early Sensation' are stunning, seen against finely cut, dark glossy green foliage. The winter-flowering *C. cirrhosa* has a cream base to its freckled interior, while the spotless 'Jingle Bells' is the closest this species comes to pure white. The evergreen *C. armandii* is white and in its 'Apple Blossom' form the buds are pink but, once opened, they fade to white in full sun.

Among the atragenes are white forms of *C. alpina* and *C. macropetala* but these are less vigorous than their parents. Their foliage is a touch anaemic, which gives them a kind of pallid refinement. *C. montana* is mostly white in the wild; var. *grandiflora* and var. *wilsonii* were also both wild-collected forms. White is also plentiful in the early large-flowered hybrids, the variation lying in the stamen colour, cream in 'Marie Boisselot' and maroon in 'Miss Bateman'.

C. potaninii, one of the best of the wild white species with small, simple four-petalled flowers, has been used in several new crosses. With *C. heracleifolia* it produced 'Sander', a sprawling herbaceous plant with scented white stars; with *C. tangutica* the result was 'Anita'; with *C. rehderiana* it produced 'Jasper', and with *C. vitalba* it resulted in 'Paul Farges', a fantastically vigorous plant for late summer.

The texensis group and the viticellas sport a few white varieties. 'Kaiu', a beautiful new hybrid from Estonia, has hundreds of small white bells with tinges of light violet. 'Alba Luxurians' is the commonest white viticella in commerce.

PINK Pink and pinky mauve are common among the large-flowered hybrids, often embellished with bars and stripes, highlights or a darker reverse. 'Comtesse de Bouchaud' is probably the best pink all-rounder. 'Markham's Pink' and 'Ballet Skirt' are beautiful spidery forms of the atragene *C. macropetala*.

C. montana has some naturally pink forms. The original introduction was called 'rubens', though this has been superseded by an array of new forms, some of which, like 'Warwickshire Rose', have larger flowers and darker leaves. Most pinks tend to stand out well against shadier walls.

BLUE, MAUVE AND PURPLE Most of the original large-flowered hybrids from the nineteenth century ranged from white through pale lavender to purple. The deep purples probably originated from *C. viticella* and *C. integrifolia* and the paler colours from *C. patens* and *C. lanuginosa* – hence pale blues are more common among early-flowering and dark purples among late-flowering hybrids. This colour range is certainly the easiest on the eye and most straightforward to place in the garden. The paler colours should be planted in shade to retain their depth.

Blues and purples are absent in evergreen clematis as well as the orientalis and montana groups but readily available in all others. The closest to true blue is the large-flowered 'Fujimusume', while 'Mrs Cholmondeley', 'William Kennett' and 'Will Goodwin' are all rewarding, as are the later-flowering 'Perle d'Azur', 'Prince Charles' and Blue Angel. The best of the darker blues are 'Lasurstern' and 'Lord Nevill', although my favourite is the inky-blue 'Rhapsody'. The tried and true 'Jackmanii' is peerless, while 'Warszawska Nike' is the most reliable in the red-purple range. The rich and velvety 'Royal Velours' and 'Black Prince' are among the darkest of all purples and in a dull light can appear almost black. Take account of this when placing them against a wall or growing through a host plant.

RED Red hybrids, descended from *C. texensis*, are mostly late-season bloomers and resemble the various shades of red wines. 'Niobe' is one of the best dark claret-reds, fading to deep ruby, while 'Westerplatte' improves on this in intensity but is a less strong grower. There are many dull reddish-purples whose colours are often

RED, PINK, BLUE AND PURPLE (opposite)

1 *'Madame Julia Correvon' is a deep wine-red viticella, the well-veined sepals twisting and curving with age to give it a looser, more open look. Raised in France by Morel, pre-1900.*

2 *'Blue Bird' differs from* C. macropetala *in that its sepals are a paler slate-blue and twisted. With their neat, fine-leaved growth, beautiful spring flowers and seedheads, all the atragenes are well adapted to growing on walls. Reaching to only 3–4m, they are also easily trained, given a simple network of wires. The macropetalas are just as at home against a dry, sunny wall as on one that is cold, damp and shady. Raised in Canada by Frank Skinner, 1962.*

3 *One of the most popular hybrids among breeders and gardeners, 'Lasurstern' is also one of the best blues. The neatly overlapping deep lavender-blue sepals have wavy margins and taper to a fine point; they fade to blue-violet in the centre. This reliable variety is vigorous to 3m and densely covered in flowers, with a second crop in late summer. Raised in Germany by Koos and Koenemann, 1905.*

4 *Soft pink is rare among clematis but 'Pastel Pink' is the gentlest shade of sugary pink. Most large-flowered hybrids with pale pink colouring fade quickly in sunlight but in this form of* C. integrifolia *the colour is sustained.*

diminished by age and strong sunlight but which still look lovely in the garden. 'Ernest Markham', 'Madame Édouard André', 'Rouge Cardinal', 'Rüütel', 'Madame Grangé', 'Ville de Lyon' and Vino are the best of these.

'Madame Julia Correvon', the earliest viticella to flower, is a strong pinky red, while 'Kermesina' is a darker, purer red. Perhaps the closest of all is the tulip-shaped 'Gravetye Beauty' (see page 13). 'Sir Trevor Lawrence', another texensis type, is a rich reddish purple with a deeper red bar, a characteristic it must have inherited from the purple large-flowered 'Star of India', one of its parents.

The striping of clematis is mostly found in the large-flowered hybrids, and those closely related to *C. patens*. The all-time favourite is 'Nelly Moser', pale pink with a deep pink bar, a striking contrast lost in bright sunlight. 'Lincoln Star', 'Bees' Jubilee' and 'Doctor Ruppel' have similar colour make-up, while 'Fireworks' and 'Mrs N. Thompson' have stronger colouring, with purple sepals and bright bars.

foliage and seedheads

Few gardeners would choose clematis on the strength of their foliage alone but many are well worth growing for their leaves as well as their flowers. Particularly when grown on a house wall, it is essential that a plant should look well dressed when it is not in flower. Their abundance of fresh, finely cut leaves which remain fresh after flowering makes the spring-flowering atragenes eminently suitable for furnishing house walls and garden fences. The downfall of the large-flowered hybrids and viticellas is that they can often look singularly tatty and sad after they have flowered. But it is possible to camouflage this tattiness by growing them beneath a canopy of roses or through other, more handsome wall shrubs.

The evergreens are seductive, exactly because they are evergreen. *C. cirrhosa* looks good in winter, especially in the fern-leaved form var. *balearica*, but it is as well to be aware that this clematis loses most of its leaves in midsummer before refurnishing itself before the autumn. The New Zealanders, with few exceptions, are evergreen, and many have fresh, dark green foliage which is both glossy and finely cut. For those who are fortunate to live in an area where it grows well, *C. armandii* fulfils the demands of gardeners who want a fragrant evergreen climber. Its relatively large leaves are, however, rather vulnerable to cold, drying winds, which can burn and tear them, but where they are given shelter they are lustrous and bold. For this reason they are especially suited to being grown against a sheltering wall in small town gardens.

The dense growth and vigour of *C. montana* make it useful for covering unsightly sheds and other buildings and the new leaves of many forms are an attractive purple-bronze. This colouring is most pronounced in the variety 'Warwickshire Rose' and, to a lesser extent, in 'Tetrarose', 'Freda' and 'Vera'. Some forms of *C. chrysocoma*, as well as a hybrid between this species and *C. montana* called 'Dovedale', have fine red autumn colour, a trait for which clematis in general are not renowned.

The purple young growth of the herbaceous *C. recta* 'Purpurea' has been prized for inclusion in large flower borders since the days of Gertrude Jekyll, who sang its praises. Be warned, however, that this variant is often grown from seed and some forms revert to green much too early in summer. *C. recta* 'Velvet Night' is a form that should be sought for its rich, translucent red-purple foliage which is as good as that of *Cotinus coggygria* 'Royal Purple' or a purple-leaved berberis. If you cut down *C. recta* after its first flush of white flowers in early summer, it will renew itself, keeping its purple colouring until later into the season. The few clematis which have glaucous or blue-green leaves may be worth choosing for

LEAF INTEREST (opposite)

1 *The boldest foliage of all the reasonably hardy clematis belongs to the evergreen* C. armandii. *The large, handsome strap-like leaves need some protection from wind to prevent damage. It does well in sheltered town gardens with high walls.*

2 *Many forms of* C. montana *have bronze-purple young growth, which steadily turns green in summer, but this stunning variety could be grown for its foliage alone, retaining its intensity longer than other varieties, especially in full sun.*

3 *The young foliage of this select form of* C. recta *is vivid and translucent. A clone selected in the 1990s by Bob Brown of Cotswold Garden Flowers, 'Velvet Night' is still scarce in cultivation because it is difficult to raise in any reasonable number from cuttings.*

4 *Finely cut glaucous foliage is common among a number of species in the orientalis group, such as* C. tibetana *subsp.* vernayi *'Orange Peel' and* C. ladakhiana. *This form of* C. intricata, *with small orange-yellow flowers, is one of the parents of 'My Angel'.*

this unusual feature. The finely cut, glaucous leaves of *C. ladakhiana*, a member of the orientalis group with rusty orange freckled flowers, are almost beautiful enough for this clematis to be grown for its foliage alone. In the same group the original orange-peel clematis, *C. tibetana* subsp. *vernayi*, has glaucous leaves which set off its lemon-yellow flowers to perfection.

C. aethusifolia, a rare species from China, is also known as the parsley-leaved clematis for its very finely cut foliage. A number of variegated clematis have been selected over the years but none of them has been stable or hardy enough to make it into commerce. The most notable of these is the golden *C. tosaensis* 'Aurea', a form from Japan which retains green leaf veins.

SEEDHEADS

Not many garden plants can claim to have both beautiful flowers and handsome seeds, but the *Clematis* genus certainly does. Indeed, there are few more wondrous sights in an autumn garden than a mound of *C. tangutica*, *C. tibetana* or 'Bill MacKenzie', full of fluffy silver seedheads, punctuated by a few lingering yellow blooms, set against the flame-red leaves of other climbers like *Vitis coignetiae* or shrubs such as *Euonymus europaeus* or callicarpa with its bright purple berries.

Most of the orientalis group put on a fine display of seeds and, when enlivened by the sharp slanting light of autumn, it would be no exaggeration to say that it is worth growing this group of clematis for their seeds alone. Lesser-known varieties like 'Annemieke' with small, soft yellow flowers, 'My Angel' with small bronze-and-yellow flowers, and 'Sundance', a scrambling herbaceous plant with cream-coloured blooms, are all worth collecting for their autumn display. Many of these keep their seedheads in nice condition into the new year, by which time their silveriness begins to tarnish. Old man's beard (*C. vitalba*) is well known for its winter appearance, especially in areas of chalk downland, where on frosty mornings, crystals of hoary ice cover their balls of seed.

The atragenes are the second-favourite group of clematis for their seedheads. *C. macropetala*, with blue flowers in spring, carries attractive feathery seedheads well into late summer and *C. alpina*, while it does not put on quite as flamboyant a show, nevertheless has noteworthy seeds of its own. The integrifolias are also good, in particular 'Rooguchi' and 'Fascination', while the seedheads of the large-flowered hybrids are more curious than beautiful. In many the individual seeds, which have hairy tails, curl around each other to make an intricate spiral ball. While not contributing to the overall beauty of a garden, these intriguing sights, encountered while investigating plants more closely, all add to the joy of gardening.

The individual seedheads of the large-flowered hybrids (above) are a curious bonus.

This close-up detail (opposite) of a seedhead of the herbaceous C. recta 'Purpurea' shows up the feathery styles that connect to the ripening fruit.

The little known 'Sundance' (left) has small, starry cream flowers in summer that transform into the lightest of silver seedheads, which persist from late autumn deep into winter. They are seen here in a happy association with the violet berries of Callicarpa bodnieri 'Profusion'.

ways of growing

Travelling as they can in almost any direction, clematis offer countless opportunities for stunning and surprising effects in the garden. Whether grown into trees, through shrubs and roses or simply against walls, fences or sheds, their graceful wanderings and their exceptional diversity of sizes and colours add another dimension to garden planning. Even if tucked in as an afterthought, as they so often are, they can still give an aesthetic lift or a dramatic twist to almost any style of garden.

The ideal spot for C. armandii *(above) is in the crutch of two walls, safe from cold winds, perhaps near an entrance where its sweet fragrance can be savoured. For some, the variety 'Apple Blossom' does not have quite enough flower power or strength of colour but I love its pink buds that open paler pink and fade to white.*

In mixed borders of herbaceous perennials and shrubs, some clematis can be left to dart about at will. Smaller shrubs, like lavender, caryopteris, spiraea and potentilla, can act as anchors or bases from which clematis such as the Estonian 'Kaiu', with its long shoots and small nodding white bells (opposite), can make surprise forays into the neighbouring perennials throughout summer.

Lightweight in growth and with a natural climbing habit, clematis are the obvious choice to decorate vertical surfaces. And by far the most obvious growing position is flat against a wall or solid fence. Showy and bold, the extrovert large-flowered varieties will flower profusely on most walls, with all their blooms facing the same direction and almost smothering the entire plant. However, house and garden walls are precious commodities and a plant given such pride of place must return the compliment by looking good all year round.

Among the few plants that can live up to this expectation are some clematis, but unfortunately the most flamboyant – the large-flowered hybrids – fail the year-round test. When not in bloom their garb is dowdy and frequently downright ugly, especially when grown alone. The foliage can mysteriously turn brown after flowering, and both the dead leaves and old flowerheads may hang on persistently unless they are removed.

The sturdy spring-flowering atragenes, with their habit of sprawling over mountainous rocks, are particularly well adapted for walls. They are attractive when out of flower, with their fine foliage and silvery seedheads, and will even generously sport the occasional out-of-season bloom. Both alpinas and macropetalas are unlikely to outgrow a house wall, rarely exceeding 3–4m in height, and need little pruning or training. Along with the well-foliaged and equally suitable *C. armandii*, *C. montana* and clematis in the orientalis group, all the atragenes can be pruned back after flowering if they get out of hand.

Always consider the aspect of a house wall, a boundary wall or a fence before choosing a clematis to clamber up it.

SUNNY WALLS

Warm, sunny walls offer great opportunities. Apart from reflecting sunlight, those constructed in brick and stone can store heat during the day and act like a storage heater, lifting the night temperature against the wall by a degree or two. This may be significant enough to allow you to experiment with one or two of the more tender clematis, like the New Zealanders, which you might not normally credit with being hardy enough in your area.

In a secluded corner by a doorway I would always give priority to *C. armandii*, the most handsome of clematis for its evergreen leaves and delightfully fragrant white flowers in early spring. Although quite hardy, its young, unfurling bronze-tinted growth is prone to being shredded by the cold, drying winds that can whip viciously around corners or across the face of a wall. Another popular evergreen, *C. cirrhosa* has bell-like flowers in winter, its buds and open flowers able to withstand at least -6°C unscathed. In the best forms, such as var. *balearica* and var. *purpurascens* 'Freckles', the flowers are speckled inside, a trait that needs to be admired from below. Once established, both these vigorous species need a width of 4–5m of wall on which to fan out.

Other lovers of growing on hot, dry walls are *C. flammula* and its offspring, *C.* × *triternata* 'Rubromarginata'. Place them where their powerful summer fragrance can waft over a path or doorway.

SHADY WALLS

The majority of clematis, apart from those mentioned above, will grow happily against a shady, sunless wall or one that receives only an hour or two of sunshine. For some, this may actually be a preferable position, the atragenes being the most suitable for very cold, exposed walls and fences under 3m high. A large-flowered hybrid with a pale colour and pale stripes, like the old favourite 'Nelly Moser', will retain its colour on a shady wall whereas in full sun its pink bars are rapidly bleached out. Pale blue and mauve varieties, like 'Silver Moon' and 'Twilight', suffer in the same way, losing all their subtlety within days of exposure to bright sunlight, as will the creamy Wada's Primrose, 'Moonlight' and 'Guernsey Cream'.

Apart from favouring intensity of colour, a shady wall will often help clematis to flower later and for longer. Too much shade, however, can deter some of the deeper red clematis, like 'Gravetye Beauty', from flowering. Beware of letting clematis grow right to the top of shady walls on a garden boundary. They may, when discovering more light on the other side, reach over and turn their gaze towards your neighbour! Shady walls will also tend to entice a clematis upwards, discouraging it from flowering on its lower stems, a complaint often encountered in some early large-flowered hybrids, like the pure white 'Marie Boisselot'. There is little you can do except re-train the shoots horizontally as they grow or unhook them when they reach the top and let them hang back down again.

HEIGHT

Garden walls and single-storey house walls need a clematis that will grow no more than 2–3m tall. None of the large-flowered hybrids, the atragenes and the texensis group will exceed this but if you choose montanas and orientalis types, you should prune and train them (see pages 138–41). If height is limited, montanas can be pruned immediately after flowering to contain them, but they should still be given a width of at least 5m of wall to perform at their best. In one of her books, Gertrude Jekyll shows a montana growing against a barn wall, attached at one or two points at 2m intervals, so that it hung in elegant swags in between.

'Blue Bird' (above) thrives in the shady corner between two house walls. All the atragenes are well adapted to wall culture and can be left unattended for years, although an occasional hard pruning after flowering will invigorate them, especially when accompanied by generous feeding.

When *C. montana* is grown on a wall more suited to its height of 4–5m, it will need little care, although it would benefit from thinning out the old wood every few years (see pages 138–41). I would choose a variety like var. *rubens* 'Odorata', var. *wilsonii* or 'Fragrant Spring' for the bonus of fragrance. Once you have savoured their sweetness, other montanas, superb as they may be, will tend to disappoint in the same way that some non-scented roses and dianthus do.

'Bill MacKenzie', one of the orientalis group of clematis, is a handsome candidate for a wall, with its extended flowering season and long-lasting seeds. This and 'Lambton Park' can produce festoons of growth which, if the main stems are secured, will hang down in spectacular curtains. Although these are late-flowering clematis, which are normally hard pruned, you need only cut them back as far as their main stems and the emerging shoots in early spring. If after a year or two their old growth becomes thick and matted, the old stems can be cut down as drastically as you wish. Cutting back these later-flowering clematis, including viticellas and some of the species, can prove challenging – you may well need a stepladder – and the harder you prune, the later they will flower.

THE COMPANY OF OTHERS

Although I have warned against growing large-flowered hybrids alone on walls, I would certainly allow them to trail through other wall shrubs, climbers and roses to camouflage their out-of-flower shortcomings (see pages 44–47). The dense but attractive growth of *C. armandii*, *C. cirrhosa* and the atragenes may be too much to drape over delicate wall shrubs but other climbers, like the vigorous wisteria, honeysuckle or trumpet vine (*Campsis*), will cope well with the competition.

The presence of ivy on walls will make the soil dry and inhospitable. Where clematis do manage to grow with ivies, pay attention to the choice of flower colour. Some pink clematis will clash unpleasantly with gold-variegated forms of ivy, but would look infinitely better against a silver-variegated form like *Hedera helix* 'Glacier' or plain dark green ivy. Popular evergreen wall shrubs like ceanothus, pyracantha and *Garrya elliptica* would all happily play host to the large-flowered hybrids. Some late strands of a Jackmanii hybrid can bring a surprising bonus alongside the orange or red berries of pyracantha or cotoneaster, while a spring-flowering ceanothus could be enhanced by the double-flowered 'Proteus'.

With or without companions, before considering planting clematis against a wall (see page 136), look carefully at the condition of the soil at its base, where it can be deficient in nutrients and moisture. If the soil is dry and powdery, the overhang of the house eaves or coping may be preventing rain from falling there. Soil texture is crucial for the roots of plants, which need to travel with ease in their search for sustenance. While poor soil texture is hard to improve, you can work in rotted manure or garden compost to ameliorate its moisture-retention.

Hard pruned and with plenty of vigour, 'Perle d'Azur' (below) comes alive in late summer. Here it is allowed to scale the heavy coils of a wisteria, studding its light green foliage with violet-blue flowers long after the wisteria has ceased to bloom.

through shrubs and trees

In my role as curator of the national clematis collection (at Burford House Gardens in Shropshire, England), I often came across anxious visitors in search of more clematis. Finding very few on the walls, they would wonder where the rest could possibly be. I gently turned them away from the walls and directed them deeper into the garden where they would find more than 200 clematis hanging in roses, shrubs and trees, or threading their way through the flower borders.

To my mind, it is when they are grown through trees and shrubs that clematis truly come into their own. Using other plants to gain a foothold in their search for sunlight is, of course, how they would naturally be growing in the wild. We can emulate this to good effect in the garden, where the climbers will brighten up dark corners, furnish dull-leaved shrubs and perhaps add an extra piquancy to a lovely shrub already in flower.

Matching a clematis to a host plant, taking into consideration height, vigour, colour, preferred aspect and flowering time, becomes a fusion of art and science with almost endless possibilities. Once hooked by this matchmaking, furnishing walls may by comparison appear a very one-dimensional affair. Consideration must always be given to the weight of clematis lying over their potential host plants. *C. montana* and the atragenes create mats of growth that can obscure light from plants below them. This dense covering can even be a problem with the annual growth from hard-pruned clematis like the viticellas. Where weight threatens a host plant, the clematis should be thinned in winter and in the growing season.

FLOWERING SHRUBS

For those with small gardens, possibly with no trees or walls, growing clematis through shrubs or a hedge is a great opportunity to extend the seasons without making room for more plants at ground level. With flowering shrubs, there are two approaches. You may choose a clematis whose flowers are timed to coincide with – and complement – those of the shrub, or select one that flowers before or after the shrub, to enliven its plain appearance. Then it is a matter of fitting a suitable guest to the host, in terms of colour and vigour as well as flowering time.

Consider first the individual merits of the potential host plant – what it is like in flower and without flowers. Several spring-flowering shrubs are quite dull affairs when clad only in their leaves – lilacs, forsythia, many viburnums, deutzia, philadelphus and spiraea are just a few examples of shrubs that dress rather plainly by midsummer. There are many large-flowered clematis whose early blooms will open with those of the shrub and which will grow well through most shrubs without doing them any harm. They may also produce a flush of flowers later on.

'Paul Farges' (below), a hybrid of C. potaninii *and* C. vitalba*, is a plant of extraordinary hardiness and vigour. A prolific bloomer, starting in mid-summer, it will go on for months and here its white flowers stud the dark red leaves of* Cotinus coggygria *'Royal Purple'. Named in honour of a French missionary and plant collector, it was raised in the Ukraine Botanical Gardens in 1964.*

'Purpurea Plena Elegans' (above) is a hardy, vigorous double form of C. viticella, reaching up to 4m tall and tolerating a wide range of conditions. Its deep, dusky red-purple flowers could benefit from a foil of silver- or gold-leaved shrubs. Here it is pictured growing through a lacecap hydrangea.

Equally well-suited, and an ideal choice for later flowering, are the Jackmanii hybrids and the viticellas. The great advantage is that they will be hard pruned in winter, leaving no evidence of their presence in spring, while the shrubs are flowering. (But you can leave the lower stems attached to the shrub unpruned, to give the new shoots a headstart each year.) The clematis will surreptitiously gain a foothold in spring, as the shrub's flowers start to fade, and will appear later on in summer out of the sides or top of the shrub. There is a joy to this late appearance of a clematis, especially if it is one that you planted a few years earlier, now soaring into view. I once returned after a summer holiday to find a lilac that appeared, from a distance, to be flowering for a second time. On closer inspection the lilac was covered in the pink flowers of 'Abundance', a viticella planted two years earlier.

Late-flowering shrubs like buddleja or *Hydrangea paniculata* make excellent hosts for *C. viticella*. These shrubs are usually hard pruned in winter and, while an early large-flowered hybrid might look lonely flowering in a bush of hard-pruned twigs, a viticella, Jackmanii or taller herbaceous clematis like *C. × diversifolia* and its cultivar 'Heather Herschell', or 'Alionushka', will bush up and flower with their host. This end-of-summer display is often welcome in gardens with little zest left in them. It can be played out on a lower level with lavenders, caryopteris or dwarf roses, using smaller forms of *C. integrifolia* or a texensis-group clematis.

FOLIAGE SHRUBS AND EVERGREENS

Clematis can be planted to grow through evergreens and shrubs with coloured foliage to great effect. Variegated shrubs or those with purple, gold or silver foliage are all prime candidates for enhancement. The variegated *Cornus alba* 'Elegantissima' or *Rhamnus alaternus* 'Argenteovariegata' will look superb studded with an early-flowering dark red clematis like 'Ernest Markham' or 'Westerplatte', or a late-flowering dark purple form like 'Jackmanii Superba'. For a lighter effect, try the pale blues of 'H. F. Young' for an early flower, or Blue Angel for later on.

Pale blue and purple clematis like 'Perle d'Azur' and 'Gipsy Queen' show up brilliantly in silver-leaved trees and shrubs, like the weeping pear (*Pyrus salicifolia* 'Pendula') and *Elaeagnus* 'Quicksilver'. Curiously, the same clematis that looks joyful in variegated and silver shrubs will look sumptuous in purple- and bronze-leaved shrubs like *Cotinus coggygria* 'Royal Purple' or *Cercis canadensis* 'Forest Pansy'. White-flowered clematis also show up well in these dark-leaved shrubs, especially the large-flowered 'Miss Bateman' whose purple stamens reflect the shrub's leaf colour.

Purple and dark blue clematis look stunning weaving through gold-leaved shrubs. The golden forms of cotinus, cornus and philadelphus all tend to turn quite green by late summer, so for the most startling effects choose clematis whose flowers coincide with their earlier, brighter foliage. Examples might include dark purple large-flowered clematis like 'The President' or 'Beauty of Worcester', an atragene like 'Helsingborg' or, in the red-purple spectrum, 'Sunset' or 'Niobe'. *Catalpa bignonioides* 'Aurea' can be kept as a tree or pollarded each year to behave more like a shrub. Either way, it will look bright well into the summer and a late viticella such as the deep red-purple 'Royal Velours' will conjure up a rich mix. White and pink flowers look less effective against gold.

IN TREES

Gardeners will often – out of sentiment, or the need for shade or privacy – keep mature old trees that are well past their best. It may be a shapely old apple tree but could equally be a wizened Christmas tree or a row of cypresses that are dull and heavy on the eye. Clematis, alone or with rambling roses, can transform even these seemingly lifeless towers of dusty green into cascades of flower. Since old conifers tend to make the soil dry under their canopies, plant the clematis 1–2m outside their 'drip line', then train it over the ground or up a cane to reach the tree.

A few large-flowered hybrids and the atragenes are vigorous enough to reach into smaller trees that have low, forking branches, such as small maples or magnolias – or they can at least hook on to their lower branches and hang out in the crutch of their boles. They may need help to reach the lower branches but any supports used will soon be covered by growth. The alpinas and macropetalas can reach up to 4m if well-fed, and their growth will do the host tree no harm. Small trees like apples, pears or sorbus make excellent hosts, whereas cherries have too vigorous a root system for smaller clematis to contend with.

For bigger trees like oaks, large maples and a number of evergreens, the vigorous *C. montana* comes into its own, its white or pink flowers draping the canopy in spring. This may be too vigorous for crab apples which bloom at about the same time. However, if this is a combination you cannot resist, prune the clematis quite hard straight after flowering (see pages 138–39) to stop it throttling the tree. Avoid trees with dense root systems, such as beech, as hosts for clematis.

Late-flowering clematis, including species like *C. potaninii, C. vitalba, C. terniflora* and those in the orientalis and tangutica groups, are also suitable for growing into trees. 'Bill MacKenzie' has attractive yellow bells in late summer and autumn, but my favourite is 'Paul Farges', a hybrid between *C. potaninii* and *C. vitalba*, whose long wands of growth sprout small white flowers all summer.

CREATING COMBINATIONS

Like childhood sweethearts, shrubs and clematis planted within a year or two of each other can live happily together for years. The clematis must be given its own space to develop rather than being tucked into the base of a host, where it will thirst and starve. It is harder to force a young clematis into an older and well-established tree or shrub, because the competition for root space, moisture and nutrition is a lot tougher. Bearing in mind the wayward and often contradictory nature of these climbers, you may need to consider the direction in which a clematis will tend to grow. A clematis will always search for the light, so despite your best intentions it might end up reaching into a taller neighbouring plant. Equally, when you plant a clematis on one side of a shrub, it is quite capable of growing right through to the other side and flowering there instead.

growing with roses

It is a great blessing that two of the most beautiful and deservedly popular of all garden plants look wonderful together, while also sharing virtually the same cultural needs. Roses and clematis are a match made in heaven and bringing them together makes for an exciting bit of horticultural theatre.

These two favourite plants are very similar in their needs for water, food, pruning and pest control. They both require plenty of moisture in the growing season and benefit from a good dose of rotted manure placed around their roots in autumn (see Feeding and watering, page 144). Roses and clematis can be pruned at the same time, with an autumn tidy-up and some heavier pruning in late winter. After the first flush of roses in summer, deadheading will always improve the chance of later flowers on both the roses and the clematis. And for those who spray their roses for the control of pests, or diseases like mildew, both plants can receive a simultaneous dose (see Pests and diseases, page 146).

CHOOSING PARTNERS

The framework created by the stems of shrub or climbing roses makes an ideal climbing frame for all the large-flowered hybrids as well as the lankier herbaceous clematis and the less vigorous viticellas. Matching a rose with a clematis involves a few careful considerations regarding height, vigour, colours and flowering times.

LARGE-FLOWERED HYBRIDS

If you are a novice at this kind of horticultural dating, I recommend that you start by pairing the larger of the shrub roses that grow 1–2m tall with the one of the later-flowering Jackmanii-type clematis. This will allow the rose to flower in its main season, unencumbered, while the clematis steadily threads its way through, to emerge among the rose's late-summer blooms and hips. In winter, the clematis can simply be pruned to the ground when you are cutting back the rose (see page 140).

Many old-fashioned shrub roses flower only once, in early summer, but they are often of quite strong constitution, especially the Alba, Gallica and Damask roses. Although they can look wonderful with an early large-flowered clematis, the rose's less than attractive late-summer garb would be greatly improved by the blooms of a later flowering clematis. Roses such as *Rosa rugosa* 'Alba', 'Céleste', 'Madame Hardy' or *R. gallica* var. *officinalis* would all lend support to a clematis like the reddish purple 'Gipsy Queen' or the blue 'Prince Charles'. The late-flowering Jackmaniii types – Blue Angel, 'Victoria', 'Perle d'Azur' and 'Jackmanii' itself – would also be perfect for weaving through groups of roses.

The flowers of 'Madame Julia Correvon' open a little earlier and are larger than the rest of the viticellas. Their early season conveniently coincides with the first flush of roses in early to mid-summer (here Rosa 'Dortmund'), creating a perfect partnership of form and colour. The deeply veined sepals of this wine-red clematis twist and curve with age, giving it a loose, more open look. Raised in France by Morel, pre-1900.

The first time I saw a clematis flowering with a rose, it was a combination dreamed up by John Treasure – *C.* 'Corona' in *R.* 'Reine des Violettes', where the two colours were only a shade or two apart. I have repeated a similar colour scheme using *C.* 'Twilight' in the rose 'Complicata'. But when I threw 'Comtesse de Bouchaud' over the ground-cover rose Pink Bells, the colours were lost on each other, being too similar. The dusky pink of the 'Comtesse' would have blended better with purples. Though the choice of partners is vast, some winning combinations stand out. 'Marie Boisselot' and 'Gillian Blades', both pure white clematis with cream stamens, mingle beautifully with the white rose Jacqueline du Pré or with the Rugosa rose 'Blanc Double de Coubert'. 'Niobe' offers lovely rich red tones to blend with a dark Gallica rose like 'Charles de Mills'.

Most of the modern roses, especially the Hybrid Teas and Floribundas, are too small to take on a clematis, but many varieties of the new English Roses, bred by David Austin, are ideal. Combining the rugged constitution, refined fragrance and flower form of the old shrub roses with the floribundas' ability to flower all summer, these roses would be my next choice as potential hosts for clematis. Whether early or late, the flowers of the clematis are quite likely to coincide with this repeating type of rose.

To maximize the impact, one could of course choose a clematis that tends to repeat-flower as well. The large-flowered clematis that will repeat are those, like roses, that have been pruned well, deadheaded and fed. Examples include the inky blue 'Rhapsody', purple 'Warszawska Nike' or the paler blue 'Ramona', 'General Sikorski', 'Will Goodwin' and 'Mrs Cholmondeley', all toning elegantly with the soft pinks and whites of new English Roses like Sharifa Asma or Winchester Cathedral. Even a dark red clematis, like 'Madame Édouard André', can offset well against the pink of roses, because it has sufficient blue in its make-up for the colours not to clash.

The pale lilac flowers of 'Betty Corning' (below) hang and splay out graciously, floating gently over roses. In a dull light the colour is subdued but the flower no less enchanting. This clematis was found by Betty Corning on a side street in Albany, New York State, and introduced by Arthur Steffen in 1933. It is thought to be a hybrid between C. crispa *and* C. viticella.

HERBACEOUS CLEMATIS

My personal favourite clematis for growing with taller shrub roses in a border are the lanky herbaceous varieties that put on 1–3m of annual growth but have no means of supporting themselves. When allowed to romp around in the fabric of rose bushes, varieties like *C. × diversifolia* 'Blue Boy', 'Alionushka', *C. × durandii* or a new Japanese hybrid like 'Fukuzono' will flower near the end of the growth, appearing nonchalantly among the late flowers or early hips of a shrub rose. Both herbaceous and large-flowered hybrids are ideal to dress up the stems of climbing roses on a house wall, as neither roses nor clematis look their best on a wall alone.

THE VITICELLAS

The shapes and colours of the viticellas combine well with roses. Some viticellas are heavyweights and others lightweights. The growth of heavyweights like 'Étoile Violette' and 'Abundance' may be too dense to load on to smaller shrub roses unless you keep an eye on them and thin out shoots when they threaten to become overwhelming. A healthy, well-established viticella, if pruned to the ground, will send up a tower of shoots. If these are allowed to twine into each other, the clematis can tumble over under its own weight, and a small shrub may collapse under the burden. But if the shoots are separated at birth (see page 141), the viticella could effectively be woven among a bed of shrub roses. Among lightweight viticellas are 'Kermesina', 'M. Koster', 'Étoile Rose', 'Pagoda' and 'John Treasure', all infused with the blood of the gentler *C. texensis*.

A more even contest for vigorous viticellas would be with a rambler rose, where the two can be left to their own devices. For truly rampant ramblers, like *R. filipes* 'Kiftsgate' or 'Wedding Day', you might consider using their lower bare stems for a clematis or allowing a larger clematis to join them in a tree's canopy. Choose *C. montana* for early flowering and an orientalis or *C. terniflora* for a sunny aspect, with the latter's small white scented flowers opening in early autumn. I planted the white rose Mountain Snow with a late-flowering white clematis 'Anita', and in two years they have run 5m up the house wall, revelling in the company.

THE INTEGRIFOLIAS

Choosing plants to grow under the skirts of rose bushes – apart from lavender, nepeta and lamb's ears – is a bit of a quandary, so why not try *C. integrifolia*? Although not of the neatest constitution, with its floppy habit and flattened mass of growth in the centre, it can, if planted 50cm away from the border's edge, send the tips of its shoots into the lower stems of roses. In its wild state this clematis is blue with twisted, bell-shaped sepals, but it also comes in white and pink. 'Arabella', which behaves much like an integrifolia but will more obligingly grow up into a rose, resembles a miniature version of a bluish large-flowered hybrid.

in borders

Apart from walls and shrubs, including roses, there is a less obvious dimension for clematis to roam: the horizontal territory among herbaceous perennials.

I once grew the violet-purple clematis 'Viola' in a purple cotinus, but one year it came unhooked from the supporting shrub. Rather than risk breaking it, I left it in a heap on the ground, clamping a few shoots in place with loose stones. This plant caused quite a stir, as did a container planting of 'Pink Fantasy' which, having slipped down its canes, spreadeagled itself over the surface and down the sides of its pot. In both cases I was asked whether these were special ground-cover types of clematis. The answer is that there is no such thing but one could, in theory at least, try this with almost any clematis. But if you choose to let a clematis lie on the deck, then there it must stay, as any vertical growth will steal the flowering away from the flat plane.

There is a major caveat to this mode of cultivation: the threat from slugs, mice and snails. Even on a wall these pests will strip clematis shoots and flowers, and growing them on the ground offers them all the shelter they need. Use bushy twigs or a wire cage to keep the plant from having direct contact with the soil, and scatter sharp grit around the plant to deter slugs from crawling over it.

On a large scale *C. montana* can be used as ground-cover, where it will tend to grow into a mound several metres across. Christopher Grey-Wilson waxes lyrical over an orientalis group clematis, 'Helios', that enjoys staying on terra firma.

For much of the year C. tubulosa 'Wyevale' (left) makes healthy ground-covering clumps of bold, coarse foliage before sending up its flower spikes in mid- to late summer. This form has larger flowers than the type and carries deliciously perfumed blue flowers. It associates well with other border perennials that need room to expand, like rudbeckias and, here, Geranium 'Ann Folkard'.

In a conventional flower border, some herbaceous clematis can be left to fall about among sturdy perennials like asters and perovskia, or to droop over low retaining walls. Given a framework of twigs or pea-sticks to weave among, *C. integrifolia* will grow to 1m tall. Pea-sticks or herbaceous plant supports will also be needed for *C. recta*, a taller herbaceous clematis; *C. recta* 'Purpurea' is equally strong and has electrifying dark purple foliage in its better forms. It is good practice, as with many early-summer perennials, to cut *C. recta* down immediately after flowering.

Herbaceous clematis like *C. tubulosa* and *C. heracleifolia* are unusual in that they are self-supporting perennials, with an almost shrubby base. These plants form large clumps that can be easily divided to create weed-smothering colonies. Equally at home at the edge of a woodland garden or in a flower border, they are easy in both sun and light shade. They associate well with other late-summer perennials like heleniums, crocosmias and Japanese anemones. One or two of their hybrids have a more sprawling habit. 'Mrs Robert Brydon' and 'Praecox' have pale mauve flowers, the latter forming a dense ground-covering mass of shoots 3–4m across. Some neighbouring shrubs may be tough enough to fend off its eager advances, or the ground around it may soon become bare. This group of clematis are all cut back hard in winter, leaving a bare patch that can be planted with spring bulbs which will be dormant by the time the clematis re-grows.

Texensis-type clematis like the pale pink 'Duchess of Albany' and the superb deeper pink 'Princess Diana' will show off well in the powder-blue plumes of *Ceanothus* 'Gloire de Versailles'. From this vantage point they can drop down into sedums or perovskias or clamber through the stems of echinacea and phygelius.

C. integrifolia *(above), native to central Europe, is a lax herbaceous plant that will flop around and lean on neighbouring border perennials, like this biennial* Eryngium alpinum. *Using pea-sticks and twigs,* C. integrifolia *can be 'lifted up' to about 1m.*

If you like tidy flower borders you will need to stake C. recta *with a number of canes or a dense support of pea-sticks. Unstaked, it will collapse, especially on fertile soils. 'Peveril' (right) is a neater, more upright clone, more or less self-supporting to 1m. In early summer the clouds of small white flowers, which can be scented, are delightful. Here it receives the support of* Eryngium giganteum, *with its spiky bracts.*

growing on supports

Clematis have a penchant for flinging themselves in almost any direction and ascending to great heights. This can be exploited to the full by offering them all manner of artificial supports. There are many clematis that will cover architectural structures like arches, pergolas, arbours and obelisks. And those with a creative bent may discover a new use for less conventional materials. Scaffolding poles, tree stumps, concreting mesh and old washing lines could all be a suitable support for a tumbling or scaling clematis, as long as it can get an initial toe-hold.

OBELISKS, WIGWAMS AND CANES

When a garden design is in need of a vertical statement, an obelisk provides an alternative to a clipped or conical evergreen. Made of timber, ornate wire or wrought iron, obelisks can be elaborate and beautiful pieces of garden furniture in themselves. In winter a combination of obelisks and evergreens will lend structure to a flower garden that might otherwise be a flat expanse of twigs. In a more formal garden, with bold evergreens as a backdrop, obelisks can be placed to add rhythm and punctuation to the winter scene, but in late summer this formality will be softened by the often rather casual dress of the clematis. Regular tying, training and pinching out the tips of shoots can help to keep these climbers more or less where you intend them to grow. If you choose a late-flowering clematis, all the growth can be pruned off in late autumn to reveal the handsome structure of the obelisk underneath (see Pruning, page 138).

Different in style, a wigwam is often a home-made affair consisting of a group of poles or bamboo canes pushed into the ground in a circle and pulled and tied together at the top. The tie can itself be made more interesting by using sisal, woven twigs or leather laces. If the poles are thick, the clematis will be unable to twine around them and will need a web of wire or string to grab hold of. Makeshift wigwams can be stored away in winter if they host a late-flowering variety that is hard pruned in late autumn.

For an even more casual style of support, you can push bunches of bare pea-sticks into the ground. These branches, best cut from hazel bushes, complete

A neat little box-edged parterre sits in the middle of a kitchen garden, surrounded by asparagus and potatoes (below). The obelisk is dressed with two early summer flowering clematis, 'Nelly Moser' and 'Niobe', accompanying a pink climbing rose and underplanted with penstemons. The punctuating formality of the obelisk forms a lovely contrast with the casual habit of clematis.

In the garden at Great Dixter (above), a late summer flowering 'Kermesina' soars with abandon off the top of a pole encased in wire, overlooking the purple-leaved cannas and banana tree of Christopher Lloyd's exotic garden. While striking a slightly incongruous note, clematis can readily play a part in brash and bold adventures among brightly coloured tropical plants.

with their twigs, are a popular way of growing sweet peas, which have a similar habit to most clematis. Make sure that the pea-sticks are in place before the new clematis growth emerges in early spring. Clematis grown on pea-sticks will require very little in the way of training.

CHOOSING A CLEMATIS

The smallest clematis suitable for obelisks and wigwams are the herbaceous kinds, such as *C. integrifolia* and 'Arabella'. These can be grown on small frames, up to 1m in height, to which the clematis will need to be tied periodically. 'Arabella' is a great choice as it flowers for most of the summer, and will be hard pruned during the winter. Petit Faucon, with dark purple-blue butterfly-like flowers, also has a long season. As this group does not naturally cling, you will need a fairly dense web of wires, strings or twigs to prevent them falling away from the support.

Taller frames of 1.5–2m can be clad with a number of large-flowered hybrids with a long season, like 'Niobe', 'The Bride' and 'Warszawska Nike', or even the texensis type 'Princess Diana'. A little deadheading and cutting back after the first flush of flowers will ensure a succession of late-summer blooms.

On structures 2–3m tall, all the large-flowered hybrids and the viticellas would be suitable. At Levens Hall in Cumbria, England, there is a series of green timber obelisks covered in two of the best viticellas, 'Étoile Violette' and 'Minuet', combined with fragrant sweet peas.

UMBRELLAS

A number of clematis, like 'Marie Boisselot' and 'W. E. Gladstone', have lank stems that support a cluster of often huge blooms, very high up on the plant. This unfortunate trait can be turned into an asset by growing these out on an arbour or an umbrella structure. Umbrellas are usually a wire construction in the shape of an upturned bowl (rather like a large inverted hanging basket), secured to the top of a post. The clematis will run up the post and cascade out of the frame at the top. This technique, more often seen as a method for training weeping standard roses, will require you to tie in the top growth of the clematis around the caging. If you were able to construct an extra-large umbrella, you could plant the more vigorous *C. alpina* or even *C. montana* for a much grander cascade.

ARCHES AND TUNNELS

Arches over gateways and paths are ideal structures for adorning with clematis, especially scented kind like *C.* × *triternata* 'Rubromarginata' or some montanas. For smaller arches the atragenes would be more in scale. The Jackmanii types are the right height and, flowering mostly near the top of their 2m growth, can be

quite a sight. As they have the same needs, a rose may be grown on one side of an arch, with a clematis on the other, so that their blooms can meet and mingle at the apex. Some roses can be vicious in confined quarters so they may not be the best choice for a narrow archway. Combining clematis with jasmine and honeysuckle can add flamboyance as well as potentially extending the season, but be aware that all late-flowering clematis will need hard pruning in winter. Separating the tangled mass of these climbers for pruning may prove impossible, so an early-flowering clematis variety that requires no pruning would be a better choice.

PERGOLAS AND ARBOURS

Pergolas and arbours are similar to archways, though on a larger scale, lending even greater scope for growing clematis. These structures are frequently built to support grape vines, wisteria and roses, with clematis making great companions for any of them. Make sure you do not make an arbour or pergola too narrow or too low. While they may look beautiful when covered in the abundance of summer growth, tall people may have to crane their heads to walk under the canopy and couples will have to walk through in single file.

The fragrant, pendulous racemes of wisteria look and smell their best hanging through the roof of an arbour. Large-flowered clematis, on the other hand, tend look skywards and, on the canopy of an arbour, may be lost to sight. But when grown on the side posts or on the stems of roses and wisteria, they will fill an area usually devoid of flowers. Lanky growers like 'Marie Boisselot' will shoot off through the roof, never to be seen again – unless, of course, you look down on to them from a higher vantage point in the garden or the house.

Many climbers, such as honeysuckle, wisteria and jasmine, have quite voracious appetites and clematis planted near their roots may be in danger of starving, unless you feed them well. They will fare better if grown near the roots of roses or, better still, on their own.

Wisteria is best pruned twice a year, once in midsummer and again in winter. This would provide a great opportunity to deadhead early clematis in midsummer and prune later flowering ones hard in winter. Hard pruning does not necessarily mean taking a plant right down to the ground; if the winter has not been too severe, viticellas and orientalis types of clematis can simply be

'Jackmanii' (above) is an old-time favourite for cottage gardens, growing up to 4m over porches and arches or up poles. It flowers in late summer, when many gardens have lost their lustre, and when pruned hard can be tidied away with no fuss. This is the original hybrid raised by George Jackman in 1858.

pruned down to any re-emergent growth in the spring. If these shoots are breaking out at 2m high, for example, pruning to just above this point will save cutting out a lot of wood and will also reduce the amount of training needed later on (see Pruning, page 138).

Viticellas are particularly good subjects to mix in with other strong-growing climbers on a pergola, while orientalis types like 'Bill MacKenzie' and 'Lambton Park' will enjoy the space and freedom of a pergola where they can romp around and cascade over the sides. These are ideal if you want to cover a space quickly as they waste no time getting settled in, provided they are planted well, and can cover 4–5m² in two years. Forming quite thick mats and curtains which are easily thinned out at almost any time of year, they can be used to fill in the space while other plants, like wisteria, become established.

Beware of planting *C. montana*, another vigorous grower that is quick off the mark, with other climbers, as the weaker partners may have to yield to its superior force. Entwine it only with wisteria and those rambler roses that can match it for vigour.

Growing two clematis on a tripod (below) can be an excellent way to extend the season. Here 'Jackmanii Rubra', while providing a brilliant purple foil for 'Kermesina', will flower for a week or two longer. 'Kermesina' is probably the brightest red of all the viticella types, without growing too tall (2–3m).

GROWING TWO TOGETHER

When two clematis are planted within 50cm of each other, you should ideally select two that are from the same pruning regime – otherwise, separating them once they have got going will become nigh-on impossible. If you insist on growing an early- and a late-flowering clematis together, you will have to remove both plants from their support, lay them out on the ground and painstakingly pluck and snip at the late-flowering one, before replacing the early clematis back on its frame.

For an early-flowering partnership, you could combine the alpina 'Frances Rivis' with the cream-coloured large-flowered hybrid Wada's Primrose, or you might try two macropetalas together, such as 'Markham's Pink' and 'Blue Bird'. For later flowering, Jackmanii-type hybrids and viticellas will be happy entwined together, giving any number of possible colour combinations. Select, for example, 'Prince Charles' and 'M. Koster' for blue and pink, or the tall herbaceous Blue Rain running up the stems of a yellow-flowered 'Bill MacKenzie', or 'Huldine' with 'Étoile Violette' for a white-and-blue scheme.

fences, screens, buildings

New boundary fences and garden buildings can look quite harsh when first erected. Some clematis, especially montanas and the orientalis group, will camouflage them remarkable quickly, transforming eyesores into eye-catching vertical displays. Many of the principles behind choosing and training clematis on walls and pergolas will apply to growing them on fences and garden buildings such as sheds. Making attachments to wooden surfaces is a lot easier than to brick or rendered walls (see page 143).

Clematis need nothing more than a strand or two of wire to attach them to fences. Montanas are excellent subjects for the rapid covering of new timber-clad screens and boundaries. The form 'Warwickshire Rose' (above) has narrower sepals than most, but its deep rose-pink colour is strikingly set off by the purple-bronze young foliage. Growing to 8m, it can be pruned straight after flowering, but only if it needs to be controlled.

FENCES AND SCREENS

Solid wooden fences, usually made of overlapping boards, are often erected to screen dustbins or compost bins, to act as property boundaries, or to subdivide the garden. Often, these are not particularly attractive structures but they can be readily transformed by clematis. I would especially recommend the atragenes and, if there is room, the montanas, as these clematis flower early and require little or no pruning. In sheltered gardens, evergreen clematis like *C. cirrhosa* or *C. armandii* will provide a year-round screen of foliage, with flowers in winter or spring.

Some wooden fences are topped off with a length of trellis, giving them extra height while allowing air and light to filter through and prevent the fence from appearing too oppressive. These pieces of trellis need to be fairly strong to take a montana, which in time may constrict and rupture the small timber joints, whereas the atragenes are much lighter and of an ideal height. Large-flowered hybrids, especially fast and loose ones like the purple 'The President', the more casual blue 'Mrs Cholmondeley' or the off-white 'Snow Queen', could climb up shrubs placed in front of the fence and loop into the trelliswork above.

The early-flowering hybrids like 'Mrs N. Thompson' are generally preferable to the Jackmanii-type clematis like 'Victoria', with her semi-nodding mauve-blue flowers, as the latter will need hard pruning and untangling each year – but if late flowering is what you are after, this is not an impossible task. Trellising may make up the entire height of the screen and can be designed to be highly decorative, in which case you may not wish to hide it altogether. Later flowering clematis, which are hard pruned in winter, will leave the structure exposed for half the year, from late autumn to late spring.

Open trellis fences are similar in some ways to those made of posts and wire or swagged ropes strung between posts. A combination of late- and early-flowering clematis could be employed here, but keep them well apart to allow for their different pruning regimes. If using ropes, be aware that if the rope is much thicker than 20mm, the twining leaf tendrils may not be able to grasp it, and the clematis will need to be tied in, as will all the tall herbaceous kinds.

Finally, picket and palisade fences, as well as iron railings, can be woven with clematis, which would twine attractively through and around the uprights. Such structures can even be used as a prop for scrambling herbaceous clematis like 'Mrs Robert Brydon'. But if planted on the shadier side of a fence, this clematis will tend to throw her froth of pale mauve flowers towards the sun on the other side.

CAMOUFLAGING BUILDINGS

Old or unsightly garden sheds and garages are often in need of camouflage. Clematis are very obliging in this respect and most of them are reasonably gentle too. Climbers like ivy, with its clinging aerial roots, damage the fabric of a building, while wisteria and campsis can weave their way under tiles and around guttering, twisting them off as their growth expands. But a clematis will tend to leave the walls and roofs undisturbed. Vine eyes and wires are the least obtrusive means of fixing for buildings, especially if you use late-flowering varieties that are hard pruned. Sections of plastic or wire netting will become distorted by the twisting and turning of clematis growth and will look unattractive when they are exposed in winter.

Very vigorous clematis, most notably *C. montana*, *C. terniflora* and orientalis types, may eventually swamp small buildings if left unchecked. For a lighter touch, choose an atragene like 'Frances Rivis', with its fresh foliage, spring flowers and fluffy seedheads. Garden buildings tend be only 2–3m high, so these clematis, as long as they have a few wires to help them get going, will eventually lie in mats on a flat roof. After a few years the mat may become dense and will need thinning. As with growing clematis on walls, you could lift off the whole mass, thin and sort it out on the ground, then cast some healthy strands of growth back over the roof.

The artificial quality to the colouring of the striped large-flowered hybrids makes them difficult to place in a naturalistic setting, but for excitement the stripeys are certainly a lively bunch. There is a touch of humour in this choice of the striking 'Nelly Moser' (below) to camouflage a dilapidated old shed with a sloping roof.

growing in containers

Anyone who has been to a flower show and seen the sumptuous display of clematis in full flower will have some idea just how well they can behave in containers. For a specialist nurseryman this is a godsend as clematis, which are best planted as two- and three-year-olds, will perform well in a pot for up to three or four years. In this respect they resemble roses grown in containers – they would rather be in the ground but, if given a nutritious regime and frequent soil replacement, will go on performing well for four or five years in a container, after which it is best to discard them.

In Japanese cities, where space is limited and some homes have no gardens, gardeners stack and cluster crowds of pots outside their front doors, sometimes spilling into the street. Among the miscellany of azaleas, chrysanthemums and bonsai, there will often be a few clematis in an extraordinary array of containers. The plants look happy and well but are never particularly big, as they are usually grown pots no bigger than 3 or 5 litres, so that they remain easy to move about.

MEETING THEIR NEEDS

Clematis in pots will need more attention than those growing in the garden (see Feeding and watering, page 144). In order to perform well, most clematis need a clay pot of at least 45cm in diameter and depth. Black or dark-coloured plastic pots can get very hot in full sun, so clay pots are always preferable as they stay cooler, to the benefit of clematis roots. If possible, place the pot in shade with the head of the plant in the sun.

When filled with several litres of loamy compost, a large pot will be fairly heavy, and even more so when wet. If you are not in a position to move heavy pots around, you need to be sure that the plants in them will look good for a long time – and only a precious few clematis will do that. (For ideas, see opposite and page 155). If you can move the containers around, you could create a 'nursery' area to store potted clematis while out of flower. This will enable you to plan for a succession of clematis throughout the growing season, including winter if your garden is sheltered – or if you own a greenhouse (see Clematis for all seasons, page 26). It is a good idea to topdress the container each year, replacing the top layer of compost with fresh loam-based compost.

Clematis grown in pots will need to be supported by a framework of some kind, whether it be an obelisk, a wigwam, a wire sphere or a few sticks. A simple tripod (or multipod) of bamboo canes may be the easiest support to construct (see page 142). The canes will soon disappear under the growth of the clematis, as its twining petioles will find the narrow canes easy to clasp.

This irresistible form of C. florida is one of the most beautiful of all flowering plants. C. florida var. sieboldiana (above) is more vigorous and floriferous than the species and makes a sumptuous display on a wire frame in a large pot. As with many double clematis, the flowers last a long time, and even when the sepals have fallen away the central purple boss will persist for another week or so. It is best hard pruned so as to flower in midsummer, or late spring if grown in a greenhouse.

THE BEST PERFORMERS

The atragenes do well in large pots or tall amphora, where their long flowering stems can float down the sides, with the added bonus of good seedheads. It may even be unnecessary to move these out of sight after flowering. But they are more prone to fungal disorders when pot-grown and may need to be given a preventive drench of fungicide (see pages 146–47).

With the early large-flowered hybrids, the best choices are those that will readily flower both early and late. Varieties like 'Niobe', 'Multi Blue' and 'The Bride' will all perform impressively, especially if they are given a light pruning in winter and then cut back hard after flowering (see Pruning, page 138). Among the late-flowering clematis, it is best to avoid many viticellas and the Jackmanii group, because these clematis tend to become rangy. This is also true of the orientalis group, with the possible exception of 'Helios', a dwarf form of *C. tangutica*. Late small-flowered varieties, such as Blue Angel, 'Prince Charles' and 'Betty Corning', will behave well with some training, such as spiralling them around canes and pinching out excessively long shoots.

The texensis-type 'Princess Diana' looks superb in a container and has a naturally long flowering season. If this clematis stops flowering early enough, you can cut it back hard to promote a second flowering in the autumn. Of the herbaceous clematis, 'Arabella' and a similar new one called 'Juuli' will flower continuously until autumn, requiring nothing more than some periodic deadheading.

Container culture is the best way to ensure a reliable return from all forms of *C. florida*. These finicky beauties, while not especially tender, need a long, warm season for their growth to ripen well. Taking them into a cold greenhouse in winter will help to protect and promote the new growth, which pushes out early. By the time the frosts are over, the plants can be brought outside for the summer, where their lush new growth will reward you with a long succession of flowers. If you force them too early or if, after a summer pruning, you get a late flush of buds, you can bring them into the house and place them by a sunny window for a special performance. The New Zealand clematis also make good candidates for containers since they can be kept warm and dry in a greenhouse over winter. Dwarf varieties, like *C. × cartmanii* 'Joe' and the scented 'Pixie', may be brought on to a sunny windowsill indoors while in flower.

Growing two or more clematis varieties together in a container is fun, provided they are from the same pruning group. Although, or maybe because, I can count myself among those few ambitious gardeners that have tried clematis in hanging baskets, I remain unconvinced about this way of growing them.

'Étoile Rose' (below) makes an informal and unusual container plant, flowering for four to six weeks in midsummer. Its elegantly shaped, deep pink flowers have four recurved sepals. Classified as a viticella, from which it inherits some vigour, its ancestry also includes C. hirsutissima *and* C. texensis, *both of which have passed on their weakness for mildew. 'Étoile Rose' is equally at home in a border and an open position provides a healthier lifestyle. Hard prune in winter.*

choosing
clematis

The range of clematis show such diversity in their habit, shape, size and time of flowering that you could be forgiven for being overwhelmed by choice. Each botanical group of species brings with it another season and a more intriguing shape, and with cross-breeding the results are yet more varied forms and an even greater overlap in their flowering seasons.

Following the simplified gardener's classification described on pages 20–21, our starting point is those clematis that are evergreen as well as those that flower mostly in winter and early spring. From there, we progress through the seasons, from late spring and early summer to late summer, right up to the autumn-flowering species, many of which carry elegant seedheads deep into winter – making an almost complete cycle.

'Blue Eclipse' (left) is an atragene, with C. koreana *as one of its parents.*

the evergreens

the species

Europe: *C. cirrhosa*

Asia: *C. armandii, C. henryi* var.
 morii, C. napaulensis, C. uncinata,
 C. urophylla

New Zealand: *C. afoliata, C. forsteri,*
 C. marata, C. marmoraria,
 C. paniculata, C. petrei

The evergreens are not a group of botanically close relatives but a loose band of clematis that share the common bond of being evergreen. They all flower in winter or early spring, and can be hard pruned immediately after flowering to renew vigour and the plant's shape, but this may only be needed every few years.

If you happen to live in a subtropical or a temperate climate, where winter temperatures dip no lower than -8°C, you may be able to grow most evergreens, provided they are not allowed to become too wet in winter. Those most readily available in nurseries – *C. cirrhosa* and *C. armandii* – are hardy down to -15°C, perhaps more. In colder areas some evergreens would make excellent conservatory subjects, especially the above two and hybrids of *C. forsteri*, most of which carry sweet and fruity fragrances.

C. cirrhosa has a peculiar habit of sometimes losing its leaves in summer, only to refurnish itself later in the season. This is a throwback to its natural state where defoliation acts as a defence against drought. This habit is even more striking in a closely related species, *C. napaulensis*, which can hardly be described as evergreen because it is leafless for most of the summer, greening up for winter in time to show off its curious creamy pendulous flowers with their protruding red stamens.

C. armandii has handsome evergreen foliage and fragrant white flowers. Seedlings may produce inferior plants, so good named forms should always be sought. The difficulty in propagating this species makes it one of the most expensive clematis in nurseries.

C. cirrhosa **'Wisley Cream'** (above)
The flowers on most forms of *C. cirrhosa* are creamy white bells, 4–7cm across, produced alone or in pairs on short lateral shoots, with varying amounts of maroon freckles. The first spotless form, 'Wisley Cream' was raised from wild-collected seed by Ken Aslet at Wisley in Surrey, England, in the 1970s. Since then, 'Jingle Bells', raised by Robin Savill in 1992, has superseded it in vigour and reliability; it is a lighter shade of cream. 'Ourika Valley' is the hardiest addition, collected in the Atlas Mountains in Morocco, 1968. Its splaying sepals start off pale straw, fading to white. NO PRUNE

C. cirrhosa var. purpurascens 'Freckles' AGM 1993 (right)

C. cirrhosa is native to the Mediterranean rim and islands where it scrambles among the maquis vegetation in scrubby woodland and hedgerows. Its habitat ranges from Spain in the west around to Israel in the east, as far as Asia and parts of North Africa. As might be expected from a plant with such a wide distribution, the regional forms vary greatly in their hardiness. Like its distant cousin the hellebore, to which this form – grown from seed collected on Majorca – bears a striking resemblance, it flowers in winter and is quite sought after. All forms of *C. cirrhosa* should be planted so that the flowers are above eye level, so that one can gaze up into their bells. A porch or a pergola would be perfect. NO PRUNE

C. armandii AGM 1938 (opposite)

Native to Central and Southern China, *C. armandii* is grown as much for its bold, leathery, strap-like foliage as for its white flowers in early spring. The sweet-scented flowers are produced in clusters of a dozen or more blooms. Its selected forms, like the pure white 'Snowdrift' or pink-tinged 'Apple Blossom', are far better than seed-raised plants of the species which can often bear thin and sparse flowers. In sheltered gardens, this clematis could even be described as rampant, a two-year-old plant growing as much as 5m in its first year, but it can be hard pruned straight after flowering to keep it within bounds. NO PRUNE

C. paniculata (left)
Native of the forest margins, *C. paniculata* is sacred to the Maoris, who see its flowers as the first-born children of two stars, Puanga and Rehua. Its gleaming spring flowers, 5cm across, are dazzling against their background of dark green leaves. It grows to 4m and is hardy to -10°C. Introduced to Europe as early as 1791. NO PRUNE

C. x *cartmanii* 'Avalanche' (below)
A relatively new hybrid, 'Avalanche' inherits the beautiful white flowers of *C. paniculata* and the deeply cut foliage of *C. marmoraria*. Like all in this series, it will grow to 3m in well-drained soil and full sun, though it is hardy down to -12°C. Raised by Robin White in 1990. NO PRUNE

IN NEW ZEALAND there are 11 species of clematis, most of them more or less evergreen. *C. paniculata* and *C. forsteri* have been in cultivation for over 150 years but are confined to sheltered gardens and botanical collections, while the minuscule *C. marmoraria* was only discovered in 1973. They generally have green or white flowers, some of them highly fragrant. The different sexes are carried on separate plants, the male plants having larger and more upward-facing flowers than the smaller but more prolific female plants.

Hybrids between *C. paniculata* and *C. marmoraria* have been called *C. x cartmanii*, after the New Zealand enthusiast Joe Cartman; they include *C. x cartmanii* 'Joe' and 'Avalanche', and 'Early Sensation'. They all have elegant, dark green, dissected leaves and are smothered in white flowers in spring, sometimes flowering so much that all their energy is consumed in seed production, leaving little for new growth.

C. forsteri, C. marata and *C. petrei*, crossed with species like *C. marmoraria*, have passed on their green flowers and scent to hybrids like 'Pixie', 'Green Velvet' and 'Moonman', neat plants which are capable of filling a small greenhouse with their delicious fragrance. Greenhouse culture not only provides shelter in winter but also protects the New Zealand clematis from getting too wet. During the growing season they can live outdoors in plenty of sun where they must be kept moist; but in too closed an environment, especially under plastic tunnels, they are prone to mildew.

C. marmoraria **AGM 1993** (right)

This small suckering hummock, only 6–10cm high, was discovered in 1973 creeping about in the crevices of hard marble on two specific mountains on South Island, New Zealand. The species has been a big hit with alpine enthusiasts and, in the last decade, has been used to create a flush of new hybrids, some hardy down to -12°C. Dwarf, and well-adapted for pot culture in a cold greenhouse, these new cultivars have finely cut dark green foliage and are often smothered in greenish white flowers. NO PRUNE

the atragenes

The atragenes are so distinct from other clematis that the botanist Linnaeus originally suggested they should be given a separate genus name. They all share the peculiar trait of possessing petaloid staminodes inside the flowers. These petal-like frills are present in all the atragenes but are so prominent in *C. macropetala* as to make the flower appear like a man-made double. All the atragenes have four simple sepals that hang down like a quartered bell, occasionally splaying outwards. Most of the flowers, but especially those of *C. macropetala*, are followed by attractive seedheads. There are no hybrids between this group and any of the others.

Combining some of the best qualities of the genus, the atragenes are at once tough and relaxed, expressive and delicate, unobtrusive and resilient. Like climbing columbines, their flowering is light and refreshing in spring, with a trim finery of leaves for summer and tufts of silvery seedheads well into autumn. Neither too big nor too dainty, they are at ease in gardens, where they tolerate a range of conditions. Atragenes can be pruned, hard if necessary, straight after flowering to reinvigorate a plant. This is best done every few years to stop them becoming woody and thin.

Most of the atragenes originate from the colder, wooded mountainous regions of the planet. The frost-hardy flowers and young growth appear early in the year. Their toughness would suit gardens that are too harsh for *C. montana* and would be the spring-flowering choice in gardens unsuitable for growing the large-flowered hybrid clematis. Malcolm Oviatt Ham, who collected this group, observes that alpinas are conditioned to experience a sharp break between winter and spring and that their colours are more intense for the experience.

The atragenes are near to being as perfect a climbing plant as you could want because they grow neatly from 2 to 4m tall, the ideal height for a house wall or for hanging from the lower branches of a tree. They can be left unattended for years but, to keep them neat, should be pruned hard every two or three years.

Although not the simplest of clematis to strike from cuttings, a new plant could easily be raised from layers (see pages 149–50), or suckers carefully tweaked from close to the stem, with a small amount of root attached. These should be potted up and kept on the dry side over winter, before planting out in spring.

the species
Europe: *C. alpina, C. sibirica*
USA: *C. columbiana, C. occidentalis*
Asia: *C. chiisanensis, C. fauriei,
    C. koreana, C. macropetala,
    C. ochotensis*

'White Columbine' AGM 1993 (left)
Although *C. alpina* is blue in the wild, *C. sibirica*, an ultra-hardy, closely related species, is creamy white and the source of white in many atragene hybids. 'White Columbine', with 4–5cm long sepals, was raised from seed of 'Columbine' (*C. alpina × C. sibirica*) by Ray Evison in 1986. Many white forms have pale foliage and are less vigorous. NO PRUNE

'Willy' (right)

Unusual for an alpina, whose sepals usually hang down, the pale rose-pink sepals of 'Willy' splay out when fully open. It is a gentle colour and a lovely plant to mingle with the likes of viburnums or other evergreens such as a loosely clipped yew. 'Willy' was raised as a seedling of *C. alpina* by Peter Zwijnenburg in Holland, around 1970. 'Columella', similar but with larger flowers that are a stronger pink, may in time come to supersede this form.
NO PRUNE

'Frances Rivis' AGM 1993 (opposite)

Whether grown alone on a wall or up the bare stems of a rambler rose, 'Frances Rivis' in full flower will spread a shower of pendulous blooms. Growing to 3–4m, this elegant form has extra-long (6cm) blue sepals. The original plant was raised from seed collected in the 1960s in Tibet, from *C. alpina* or *C. ochotensis*, by Frances Rivis. There is, however, a slight muddle over this cultivar as the Dutch form, with shorter, wider and darker blue flowers, may in fact be the true one. The English form is close to 'Blue Dancer' (see pages 22–23). NO PRUNE

'Markham's Pink' AGM 1993 (above)
With its pronounced flair of petaloid
staminodes inside the flower, this variety
is to all intents and purposes a pink
macropetala that was raised in 1935 by
Ernest Markham. The fabulous rose-pink
flowers, 5–8cm across, are produced in
profusion, and could entwine happily
with those of the blue or white forms.
There are many white macropetala types,
with names like 'White Moth', 'White
Lady' and 'White Swan', but they are less
vigorous than either the pink- or the
blue-flowered forms. NO PRUNE

C. macropetala **AGM 1984** (opposite)
This exquisite species was originally
discovered in 1742 by the French botanist
Pierre d'Incarville in northern China
and Mongolia. However, it was not
introduced until the intrepid plant hunter
William Purdom found it in 'brushwood
and meadows of alpine slopes' in 1912.
His companion, the rather more famous
Reginald Farrer, wrote that 'it rambles
frailly through light bushes to the height
of two or three feet, and then cascades

downwards in a fall of lovely great flowers
of softest china-blue, so filled with
petalled processes that they seem as
double as any production of the garden'.
This wonderful plant is every bit as
good as any of its 'improved' forms; it
is hardy and happy in either sun or shade,
growing to 3–4m. NO PRUNE

'Brunette' (above)
This is a cross between *C. fauriei*, a Japanese
species, and *C. koreana* var. *fragrans*, raised by
the notable Magnus Johnson from Sweden in
1979. He did much to enhance the popularity
of this group, raising many new forms. This
must be one of his greatest successes, with its
dark brown-violet flowers, 4–6cm across,
pointed and strongly ribbed. While its main
flowering is in spring, there always seems to
be a flower or two on it at any time in the
summer. It grows to 1.5–4m. NO PRUNE

the montana group

The species of this group originate in the wilderness of the western Himalayas and eastwards through the mountains of western China and Taiwan. The best known is *C. montana*, a rampant tree-climbing clematis. Ernest Markham called it 'The Great Indian Clematis' but a fairer name would be 'The Himalayan Mountain Clematis'. Since Lady Amherst introduced it to our gardens in 1831, this climber has become so familiar that it is tempting to by-pass a description.

In the wild it is mostly a white, open flower with four simple sepals surrounding a boss of creamy white stamens, growing on a vine with deeply cut foliage that can reach to 5–8m. Part of its appeal is its purity and simplicity, which liken it to the flower of a single white Japanese anemone. Indeed, when *C. montana* var. *grandiflora* was first found in 1825, it was named *C. anemoniflora*. It also possesses the great gift of scent.

The universal stardom of this species is tempered by one shortcoming – its slight lack of hardiness. This may come as a surprise to those in maritime climates and cities, where low winter temperatures and late frosts are rare and montanas in all their forms tumble easily out of trees, fold over porches and knit themselves inextricably through trellised fences. The sad truth is that *C. montana* will be killed by anything much lower than -18°C. Vicious late frosts, when the plant is full of buds and young foliage, will also destroy that year's flowers and debilitate the plant to the point where it may never recover. Fortunately, *C. montana* is a fast grower and if a specimen has been frozen to death, a new plant could replace it and grow to the same height in three seasons.

Montanas prefer some sunshine to flower well. In their natural state they scramble over bushes and rocks in the mountains, from mixed woodlands at 1,000m up to and above the tree line at 4,000m. In more open situations *C. montana* could even be allowed to form a mass of ground-cover on banks and gravelled areas, but it looks best hung out of yews and old evergreens. In smaller trees its vigour may be overwhelming unless pruned. Pruning can be done straight after flowering or left until winter, but winter pruning will involve removing the flowering shoots for the following spring. *C. montana* is so prolific that this is not serious, especially if you want to hang only a few long threads on walls or pergolas.

Ernest Wilson collected the first pink form in China in 1900 and pink has by now outstripped white in their prevalence in nursery catalogues. A plethora of new hybrids is available in new shades of creamy yellow to deeper pink, with dark young foliage or spiky double flowers. Wild montanas are not always

the species
C. chrysochoma, C. gracilifolia, C. montana, C. spooneri

C. montana var. *wilsonii* 'Hergest'
Named after Ernest Wilson, one of the world's most prolific plant collectors, who found this late white-flowered form of *C. montana* in Western China. The variety *wilsonii* is variable in the wild, so several versions may now be in cultivation. This rarer form can trace its origins to one of Wilson's collections, discovered in the gardens of Hergest Croft, England. It flowers in midsummer, six weeks after the main montana season, and has bolder, vine-like foliage. The more common form has narrow sepals and flowers two to three weeks later. Both smell of hot chocolate. NO PRUNE

'Freda' AGM 1993 (above)

This popular form of *C. montana* var. *rubens* has two-toned cherry-pink flowers fading to a paler pink in the centre of the sepals. They are well set off by the dark bronze young foliage that emerges as the flowers open. Raised in England by Freda Deacon, 1985. NO PRUNE

scented, nor are any of the other species in the group, but those that carry fragrance do so with such strength in full sun that it carries all round the garden.

C. chrysochoma is a shorter, shrubbier plant. Its native haunts in China are open forests and shrubberies of evergreen oak, rhododendron and berberis, where it scrambles rather than climbs. Hybrids between the two species *C. chrysochoma* and *C. montana* have been called *C. × vedrariensis*, and a few pop up in catalogues. Most are worth trying, although none are fragrant. The well-shaped, white-flowered *C. spooneri* is another species which has from time to time fallen between the cracks of botanical nomenclature, and is now settling down to its elevated status as a full species.

The white-flowered *C. gracilifolia* deserves a mention, especially for anyone interested in a *C. montana* type of clematis but one that is half its dimensions in height and size of flower. It has beautiful foliage and the white of the flower is dazzlingly pure. It comes from similar haunts to *C. montana*, often growing in natural shrubberies with acers and wild roses, a tempting combination to reproduce in the garden.

'Marjorie' (left)

There has been a flush of double-flowered montanas in recent years, most of them quite spiky, like this one bred from *C. montana* var. *wilsonii*. Although they have lost the purity and simplicity that is the essence of a montana, they are a curiosity and some are quite colour-ful. A more strongly coloured double form is 'Broughton Star', and there are several white doubles like 'Jenny Keay' as well as the creamy white 'Primrose Star'. This form was found in Suffolk, England, by Marjorie Free and introduced by Jim Fisk in 1980. NO PRUNE

***C. montana* var. *rubens* 'Tetrarose' AGM 1993** (right)

A genetically altered form, using an old practice dating back to the 1950s of treating seedlings with colchicine, an extract of the autumn crocus. In this case the victim was *C. montana* var. *rubens*, whose chromosomes were modified by doubling them up to become tetraploid, hence the name. The result is a slightly larger and deeper pink than the parent flower, otherwise it behaves no differently from the average deep pink montana, but it has good dark young foliage and some fragrance. Raised at the Proefstation voor de Boomkwekerij in the Boskoop, Holland, 1960. NO PRUNE

C. chrysochoma (above)

This is a much shorter, shrubbier plant than *C. montana*. The true type is distinctive in the hairiness of its leaves and in its pink flowers, borne later in summer. One plant I have grown from a wild-collected source grows to only 1.5m, with olive-green, felty leaves and clear pink flowers in midsummer. It survives temperatures of -15°C and less, but the shoots die back to a woody stump each winter. This species, given an Award of Merit in 1936, should have a sheltered position with plenty of sun. Many plants that entered cultivation under the name *C. chrysochoma* are probably carrying *C. montana* blood, especially those that display the montana habit. NO PRUNE

large-flowered hybrids

Mystery still surrounds the true origins of large-flowered hybrid clematis. Tracing their ancestry has led to much speculation, especially as none of the original three Oriental parent species, appearing in European gardens in the mid-1800s, were what we might call pure-blooded.

C. florida was the first to arrive, from China, and how much or how little it has contributed to all the large-flowered hybrids is questionable, since the two forms available then were double and mostly sterile. *C. patens* was introduced from Japan in the form of the species and two varieties, 'Standishii' and 'Fortunei', both now extinct. On the other side of the Sea of Japan, in China, Robert Fortune also found *C. lanuginosa*, 'near the city of Ningpo. It is there wild on the hill-sides, and generally plants itself in light stony soil near the roots of dwarf shrubs, whose stems furnish it with support as it grows . . . its fine star-shaped azure blossoms . . . rearing themselves proudly above the shrubs'.

No one, in this generation at least, has seen the true *C. lanuginosa*, which has not only disappeared entirely from cultivation but also from that area in China where Robert Fortune found it in 1851. In absentia, it has been accused of being the weak link that triggered clematis wilt and perhaps its absence is a kind of admission of guilt. However, an image does emerge of *C. lanuginosa* as a stockier, hairier and longer-flowering plant than *C. patens*, which itself is tall and smoother stemmed, with more pointed and gappy flowers. *C. patens* is an altogether much stronger plant and, unlike *C. lanuginosa*, quite happy in cold, damp conditions, growing well among shrubs.

large-flowered parent species
C. florida, C. lanuginosa, C. patens

small-flowered species mixed in to inject variety in colour, shape and timing *C. integrifolia, C. texensis, C. viticella*

'W. E. Gladstone'
What this hybrid lacks in its quantity of flower it makes up for in size. The very large, pale blue flowers with red anthers can be up to 20cm across on a strong but gaunt plant growing up to 3.5m high. It is one of the latest of the early large-flowered hybrids to open, blooming at much the same time as the white-flowered 'Marie Boisselot' (opposite, above), a plant of similar habit and dimensions (both are sometimes described as mid-season hybrids). Raised by Charles Noble, c.1881.
LIGHT PRUNE

In the 1930s, Ernest Markham saw clear enough distinctions between hybrids of the *C. patens* type and hybrids of the *C. lanuginosa* type to divide them accordingly. These days, Raymond Evison prefers to divide them into early-, mid- and late-flowering, the mid- and late-flowering groups tending to have more *lanuginosa* blood. Christopher Lloyd, meanwhile, gave up on sorting the large-flowered hybrids into separate types and simply groups them all together.

The minutiae of botanical and horticultural detective work may be intriguing but what we really need to know of a plant is its size, colour, the timing of its flower, and how to cultivate it. I have therefore separated this large, disparate group into two halves, the early and the late flowerers. This makes the business of choosing a little easier, though some among the early group will produce flowers relatively late, especially if they are grown well, pruned hard or cut back by a hard winter. A few in the late group, conversely, will flower somewhat earlier if they are left unpruned. There may even be some overlap between the two groups. These ambiguous varieties are listed on page 155, but the majority fall logically into one or other of the two camps.

'Marie Boisselot' AGM 1993

One of the best loved of all large-flowered clematis, raised in France by Auguste Boisselot in 1885, from seed of 'The President'. Its flowers, up to 15cm across, are beautifully formed, their broad, widely overlapping sepals pure white, with a hint of pink on opening. Pale cream stamens enhance this purity. Vigorous and tall (up to 4m), its flowers are often produced high up, making it unsuitable for containers. It opens later than most in the group. LIGHT PRUNE

'Beauty of Worcester' AGM 1984

An all-time favourite, raised before 1886 by Richard Smith of Worcester, England, this was used as a parent of other fine doubles like 'Vyvyan Pennell' and 'Kiri Te Kanawa'. The double flowers are deep violet-blue with a hint of red, the creamy stamens being exposed in some of the less double and single blooms that open later on. Flowering can be so profuse that the plants neglect to reserve some energy for new growth, a trait that weakens the plant; deadheading and feeding would be beneficial. LIGHT PRUNE

early large-flowered hybrids

'Proteus'

This hybrid is named for its similarity to the national flower of South Africa, but Christopher Lloyd, who rates 'Proteus' among the top six doubles, suggests that it is more like a double opium poppy. Its dim and murky colours of pale violet and lilac-pink are surprisingly alluring when given a good background to lift them. The brighter coloured veins and bar, and its creamy stamens, are more obvious on its later single flowers, which are not dissimilar to 'Hagley Hybrid' or 'Margaret Hunt'. 'Proteus' is a good stayer, growing up to 3m tall. Introduced by Charles Noble, 1876. LIGHT PRUNE

The early large-flowered hybrids include the largest and most spectacular of all clematis, flowering in early summer on the previous season's growth, often with a second flush on the current season's growth in late summer and early autumn. All double and semi-double forms belong in this group, though their second flush of flowers, when produced, are usually single.

These hybrids require more care and attention than most types of clematis, especially in their formative years. Some older plants grown in good soils will settle down to give reliable displays each year with little care other than annual pruning and feeding. Apart from the differing pruning regimes for the early- and late-flowered varieties (see Pruning, page 138), all large-flowered hybrids require the same cultural conditions, although some may prefer more shade than others to retain their depth of colour (see individual captions and page 155). 'Silver Moon', 'Twilight' and 'Dawn', for example, are best grown in some shade, or on a north wall where bright sunlight cannot bleach out their subtle shades.

Generally speaking, the large-flowered hybrids do not look particularly good after their first flush of flower and so are better not grown alone, except perhaps as fleeting exhibitionists in pots that can be moved out of sight. They are far better suited to being grown through, and supported by, other plants.

Those illustrated represent the range of colour and form readily available commercially, including those that have stood the test of time. Hundreds, probably thousands, of named varieties have been introduced over the last 150 years, many now extinct. Specialist nurseries may offer as many as 300 varieties

'Mrs Spencer Castle'

The semi-double flowers of this hybrid have the unique arrangement of two layers of sepals. 'Mrs Spencer Castle' produces two or three layers of pale pink to lilac-pink sepals around a boss of creamy white stamens, the second layer being narrower, shorter and wavy. The flower, 10–15cm across, has slightly deeper coloured central bars on the sepals. Single flowers often accompany the earlier, semi-double flowers but are also produced later in the year. Grows to 2.5m tall. Raised by George Jackman, 1913. LIGHT PRUNE

'Daniel Deronda' AGM 1993

This hybrid, raised in 1882, was bred in England by Charles Noble and named after the main character and title of a book by George Eliot of 1876. Its parentage is unknown. It is a strong grower with flowers that are a striking mix of dark purple, rosy purple and paler blue markings, with cream stamens. Its spherical seedheads have a curious extra twist at the top. The first flush of flowers, in late spring, is often semi-double, with larger flowers, up to 20cm across, being produced when grown in full sun. It is best, however, to plant in partial shade to retain its subtle blend of colours. It will grow up to 3m tall. LIGHT PRUNE

from this group and each country has its tried and tested favourites. Every month I receive pictures from Japan of yet more varieties, some speckled, some with their sepals rolled back or forward, some with two-toned flowers and the odd strangely distorted double. There seems no end to the inventiveness and imagination of some modern-day breeders. However, it takes a lot to knock an old variety off its pedestal, even if an improved form does present itself.

For those of us who have to make do with just one or two of these clematis in our gardens, making the choice is simply a matter of preference for colour and shape of flower. The early large-flowered hybrids represent the greatest choice in shapes and colours. If you were particular, you could shift a shade of colour very slightly and find a variety to fit. These hybrids range in height from 1.5 to 3m, and the more compact are clearly better suited to smaller gardens and container growing. All the clematis illustrated are hardy in Zones 4–8.

The early large-flowered hybrids do not all open at once. The season may start with 'Guernsey Cream' and end with 'W. E. Gladstone' up to six weeks later, depending on the climate. Later hybrids in this group also include 'Lawsoniana', 'Ramona', 'General Sikorski', 'Henryi' and 'Marie Boisselot'. Some even overlap with the earliest of the late large-flowered hybrids, like 'Comtesse de Bouchaud'.

There is one more bonus to many early large-flowered hybrids. If they are growing well, and especially if deadheaded after the early summer flush, they will give a second display in late summer and early autumn. This is the one group that deserves a careful study of its pruning needs to ensure a good return for your efforts. Other groups are either not pruned at all or are hard pruned, whereas these are lightly pruned to maximize their flower power (see Pruning, page 138).

'Doctor Ruppel' AGM 1993

This hybrid was sent to England by a Dr Ruppel from Argentina to Jim Fisk, one of those great nurserymen who spearheaded a clematis revival in the 1970s. With flowers 14–22cm across, this startling hybrid is one of the liveliest additions to the range of stripey cultivars, brighter than both 'Nelly Moser' and 'Lincoln Star'. Grown with variegated forms of plants like *Phlox paniculata* or philadelphus, the effect, although verging on the vulgar, is almost mind-blowing. Grows up to 2m and is best in some shade to retain its colour intensity.

LIGHT PRUNE

Pink Champagne

Originally named 'Kakio', after the district in Japan where it was raised in 1971 by Kazushige Ozawa, this is one of the few clematis in this colour range, 'Asao' being another, also raised by Ozawa. The sepals are purplish pink, darkening towards the edges, with this deeper colouring threading through the veins into the paler mauve central bars. A vividly handsome hybrid, flowering well on a compact plant of up to 2.5m, its blooms would nestle well among purple berberis or silver-leaved shrubs. LIGHT PRUNE

'Lawsoniana'

From the same stable and probably the same stock (*C. lanuginosa* × 'Fortunei') that produced 'Henryi', this tall-growing hybrid was raised and introduced by Isaac Anderson-Henry in 1870. Growing up to 5m, its flowers can soar out of sight. The first flush in late spring is later than most in this group and the second flush also opens quite late in the year. The long, pointed sepals can be extremely large, 14–25cm across. They are rosy purple with darker veins but fading to leave a darker bar surrounded by paler highlights. The anthers are chocolate-coloured.

LIGHT PRUNE

'Dawn'

A beautiful pale pearly pink clematis, deepening in colour towards the outer edges of its sepals. The flower, with its contrasting red anthers, should be kept in some shade to retain the subtle nuances of colour, but perhaps allowing the evening or morning sun on just enough to light up its gentle shades. It will grow to 2m, but rarely carries any late-season flowers. It was raised by Tage Lundell of Sweden in 1960 from a seedling of 'Nelly Moser' and was originally called 'Aurora'.

LIGHT PRUNE

'Ramona'

Some confusion occurred in the naming
of this plant as it crossed the Atlantic to
New York from Holland in 1888, where it
had been known as 'Hybrida Sieboldii'.
It may indeed be a different plant.
Nonetheless it has a handsome shape,
often quite cupped before opening, as
here, with lavender–blue sepals and deep
red anthers. There is no shortage of similar
blue hybrids, such as 'Mrs Hope', 'Mrs
Bush' and 'Kasugayama', all of equal
merit. 'Ramona' has a long flowering
season, starting in early summer if light
pruned, but it can also be hard pruned for
a midsummer crop of flowers.

LIGHT PRUNE

'Gillian Blades' AGM 1993

There are few clematis whose sepals ripple
at their edges with such style as 'Gillian
Blades'. The golden stamens complement
the white overlapping sepals that are
touched with mauve at the edges. It is a
compact grower suitable for containers or
to mix with small shrub roses. A seedling of
'Lasurstern', it was raised by Jim Fisk in
1975. LIGHT PRUNE

'William Kennett'

One of the few hybrids raised by H.
Cobbett, around 1875, still in cultivation. Its
parentage is unknown, but it is occasionally
listed as a *C. lanuginosa* × *C. patens* hybrid. A
fine, sturdy and prolific plant, it is one of the
first in this group to flower. Its sepals, with
attractive crimped wavy edges, are a deep
mauvish blue with rosy pink edges; there is
a large central boss of maroon stamens. The
flower, up to 15cm across, fades attractively
in full sun but retains its deeper colour in
partial shade. Pruning is normally light, as
for most of this group, but some harder
pruning in spring will produce a good flush
of flowers later in summer. LIGHT PRUNE

'Will Goodwin' AGM 1993

Similar in shape, size and character to 'Gillian Blades' (opposite), with its wavy-edged, finely pointed sepals, this is in a lovely shade of lavender-blue with creamy yellow stamens. It is an excellent clematis for mixed plantings, especially among English roses, where it may continue flowering until late in the summer, especially if fed well and deadheaded. Raised by Walter Pennell, 1954.

LIGHT PRUNE

'The President' AGM 1993

One of the great classics, this clematis has been admired for its compact habit, reliability and long flowering period, traits that breeders have borrowed for other hybrids. The rich purple-blue flowers, with dark red anthers, are very full, the sepals overlapping well and undulating at the margins. The reverse of the flower is silvery, only noticeable when it reaches over head height, which 'The President' readily does as it grows up to 3m tall. Introduced by Charles Noble, pre-1873. LIGHT PRUNE

'Multi Blue'

The exotic-looking central mound of spiky green-tipped sepals will persist for a week or two after the single layer of navy-blue sepals that surround them have fallen away. This special kind of doubling is similar to *C. florida* var. *sieboldiana* and two new paler blue hybrids, 'Blue Light' (a sport of 'Mrs Cholmondeley') and 'Crystal Fountain' (a sport of 'H. F. Young'). 'Multi Blue', a sport of 'The President', is as reliable and strong as its parent, growing to 3m, and the doubling repeats well into late summer. Discovered in Holland by J. Bouter and Zoon 1983. LIGHT PRUNE

'Mrs Cholmondeley' AGM 1993

Neat overlapping sepals are considered by many breeders to be a satisfying trait but one of the all-time great clematis, 'Mrs Cholmondeley', has rather gappy and lax, informal flowers that can flap around in the wind. It is a beautiful and relaxed hybrid to plant on arbours and among pale pink climbing roses, where its long flowering period will be appreciated. The lavender-blue flowers, with darker veins, can be as large as 22cm across, and some among the first flush may be semi-double. Raised by Charles Noble in 1873, a cross between *C. fortunei* and *C.* 'Jackmanii'. LIGHT PRUNE

doubles and semi-doubles

The double-flowered cultivars of the large hybrids are a fantastic bunch and hugely popular. The flowers can take various forms, some reminiscent of dahlias, others more like roses, poppies or peonies. The style of doubling depends on the number of stamens that change into sepals (see page 32), ranging from the frilly mass of full doubles such as 'Proteus' (see page 78) to those with an intriguing extra layer of sepals, like 'Mrs Spencer Castle' (see page 79). Their fullness combines wonderfully with climbing roses, spring-flowering ceanothus or variegated forms of shrubs like *Rhamnus alaterna* or *Cornus alba*.

The first flowers, produced in spring and early summer on the previous year's growth, are usually double, while any later flowers are often single, though a few – like 'Kiri Te Kanawa', 'Multi Blue' and Arctic Queen – can keep up the double act until later in the year. In very cold gardens, the previous season's growth may be damaged or even killed, and the early double flowers lost. If the young buds are exposed to too much cold, especially on north walls, the opening flowers may lack their true colour, perhaps even turning out green.

Experience has shown that this group is rather more prone to wilt than most hybrids and some of them are of a weak constitution, too. Frailer hybrids, like 'Duchess of Edinburgh', should be placed in full sun, given plenty of root space and fed well. Otherwise, their cultivation and pruning is exactly the same as for the single early large-flowered hybrids.

Josephine (opposite, far right)
This hybrid was discovered in 1980 by a Mrs Hill, who apparently bought the original plant on a market stall – possibly a freak sport of 'Nelly Moser' or a similar variety. It was then propagated and introduced by Raymond Evison in 1998. I find this colour and form rather vulgar, but I understand its appeal: it is as sumptuous and blowsy as an Easter bonnet. The double flowers are mauve-pink, on a compact plant growing to 2.5m. LIGHT PRUNE

'Countess of Lovelace' (left)
Her unique composition of five or six layers of neatly spaced and progressively shorter light blue sepals, topped off with a small tuft of creamy stamens, should earn this Countess a place among the aristocrats of clematis. You will, however, have to feed her well and forgive her rather casual habit and uninspiring later single flowers. Growing up to 3m or more, with flowers 10–17cm across, this hybrid is best given plenty of sun. Raised by George Jackman, 1874. LIGHT PRUNE

'Duchess of Edinburgh' (below left)

For a long time this was the only white fully double cultivar. Arctic Queen and 'Yuki-no-yoso'oi' are both whiter, looser and cooler than this Duchess. In all, the later flowers are double or semi-double. None is very strong. Raised by Jackman, pre-1874. LIGHT PRUNE

'Belle of Woking' (below centre)

The earliest fully double cultivars dominate the trade today. Jackman raised many, including this in 1875, whose silvery mauve sepals fade to silver-grey. LIGHT PRUNE

'Louise Rowe' (below right)

A lovely satiny sheen coats the pale mauve-pink sepals; their strength of colour depends on the light, time of day and age of flower. Producing double, semi-double and single flowers at the same time, a few inner sepals gracefully twist and curl around the yellow anthers. LIGHT PRUNE

'Mrs N. Thompson' (above)

With its deep violet-purple sepals, and scarlet bars that fade to a petunia-red, 'Mrs N. Thompson' is hard to beat for greatest intensity of colour. Although it is a weak grower, its frail but compact habit makes it well-adapted for container growing, where it may repeat-flower if cut back after the first flush and fed well. It was raised by Walter Pennell in 1954. 'Fireworks' has a lighter colour but is equally striking and a far stronger variety for general garden plantings. LIGHT PRUNE

'Corona' (opposite, below)

'Corona' is one of my favourite clematis for cavorting with old-fashioned roses, such as the Damasks and Gallicas. Their heights, colour and the timing of their flowers are ideally matched. Raised as a seedling of 'Nelly Moser' in Sweden by John Gudmundsson in 1955, 'Corona', like many roses, has pinky purple sepals that are set off well by crimson-purple anthers. It grows to 1–3.5m and can produce a few flowers later on in the summer. LIGHT PRUNE

'The Vagabond' (above)

A child of 'Rouge Cardinal', a late-flowering hybrid, this deep purple clematis is capable of flowering both early and late. The flowers, relatively small at 10–12cm, are liable to smother this tidy and compact plant. Raised by Ken Pyne in 1984, it is a rich mix of burgundy-purples and deep blue, with a maroon bar and contrasting cream stamens. It can be grown on any aspect. LIGHT PRUNE

'Snow Queen'

The flowers of this hybrid from New Zealand, 12–15cm across, are tinted in a silvery mauve-pink when they open, eventually fading to snow-white. Rippling at the edges, the sepals have a textured and deeply ribbed surface. For a pure white effect, it can be planted in full sun where it will soon bleach. In shadier conditions its subtle silvery shades contrast interestingly with the red anthers. A compact, free-flowering plant growing to 2.5m, it would do well in a container.

LIGHT PRUNE

Wada's Primrose

This fine clematis should be correctly known by its original name of *C. patens* 'Manshuu ki', meaning Manchurian yellow. Found growing wild in Manchuria, it was thought to be a yellow form of *C. patens*. It was given to the Japanese nurseryman Kiyoshi Wada, who introduced it to Europe under its now more familiar trade name. Its intriguing past aside, this is a lovely hybrid, a strong creamy yellow with yellow-green bars and cream stamens. The flowers, 15–18cm across, are similar to 'Guernsey Cream' but more pointed. LIGHT PRUNE

'Chalcedony'

Named after a translucent ice-blue semi-precious stone, this lovely pale blue double-flowered clematis produces flowers containing up to 60 sepals throughout the summer (unlike most double varieties). Some of the flowers that are less 'fully' double will reveal the creamy stamens. Like the similar 'Belle of Woking', it will fade to a greyish white in full sun, so is best planted in some shade. Raised by Ellis Strachen in 1976 from a cross between 'Vyvyan Pennell' and 'Marie Boisselot', it grows up to 3m. LIGHT PRUNE

'Henryi' AGM 1993

Raised by Isaac Anderson-Henry of Edinburgh, Scotland, in 1870, this is a cross between *C. lanuginosa* and 'Fortunei'. It has large white flowers, 15–20 cm across, pale green on the outside, with purple-violet to chocolate-brown anthers. It has a long flowering season and a tendency to repeat well. The downiness of its buds reflects its *lanuginosa* heritage, as does its tendency to be a rather poor starter, though it will ultimately reach 3m. It received an Award of Merit in 1873. LIGHT PRUNE

'General Sikorski' AGM 1993

This is a strong, compact and free-flowering cultivar growing to 3m, with mauve-blue flowers and hints of pink in the central bar. The early flowers are 15cm across while the later flowers, which are freely produced, are smaller. It could be hard pruned for a late display alone, but if it is lightly pruned its early flowers would time perfectly with the blooms of roses. It was raised by Brother Stefan Franczak, who named it 'Jadwiga Teresa', but was introduced from Poland in 1975 under the above name. LIGHT PRUNE

'Sunset'

Velvety red colours are rare among the
early large-flowered hybrids, though far
more common among the later Jackmanii
group. 'Sunset' is red but tinged purple-
pink, with a cerise central bar that
becomes more apparent as the flower fades.
Raised in the USA by Arthur Steffen's
nursery in the 1980s, it is a compact plant
growing to 2.5m. LIGHT PRUNE

'Fujimusume' (opposite, far left)
I am not alone in considering this to be one of the very best and truest of the blue large-flowered hybrids. The blue is light and powdery and the texture smooth and velvety, an ideal foil for pink and white shrub roses or purple-leaved shrubs. The flowers are 12–16cm across with creamy white stamens. Grow it in light shade to keep its colour, where it may reach 2.5m. Its compact habit and good branching suits it well for containers. It is best light pruned, but with its propensity for producing a good crop of later but smaller flowers, it could be pruned quite hard. Raised in Japan by Seijuro Arai, 1952. LIGHT PRUNE

'Niobe' AGM 1993 (opposite, above left)Named after the goddess of grief, this dark red hybrid is the most reliable in its colour range. The colour fades to a more purple-red. Judicious pruning, dead-heading and feeding will encourage a later crop of flowers. Beautiful with variegated shrubs and roses, it also makes an excellent container plant. Raised in Poland by Vladyslaw Noll, 1970. LIGHT PRUNE

'The Bride' (opposite)
Although raised before 1924 by George Jackman, this hybrid may have been passed over for the many white-flowered hybrids with larger flowers then available. The relatively small blooms (10–12cm) are creamy white, with creamy yellow anthers. They are borne on compact, well-branched small plants, up to 2m tall, that make 'The Bride' an ideal candidate for modern gardens and for growing in pots. LIGHT PRUNE (or prune hard for later flowering)

'Kiri Te Kanawa' (above)
Producing solid, rounded double flowers, this lovely blue-flowered clematis is a strong grower and free flowering. It was raised in 1986 from a cross between 'Chalcedony' and 'Beauty of Worcester' by Barry Fretwell, who described the 15cm flowers as 'dahlia-like'. The sporadic late-summer flowers are also double but smaller, like this one, and are rarely, if ever, single. A compact plant growing up to 2.5m, it is excellent in a container.
LIGHT PRUNE

late large-flowered hybrids

Members of this large-flowered group bloom in late summer, flowering on the current season's growth. The flowers vary from the relatively small, 8cm in diameter, to a more substantial 15cm, and are composed of either four sepals, as in *C. viticella*, or six or eight sepals. There is a predominance of rich purples and dark reds in the group; far fewer are striped than among the early large-flowered hybrids and none is double. These clematis are extremely useful in the garden for providing colour late in the summer, where they can bring a lively touch to those shrubs that flowered in spring. They can also weave among late-flowering border plants like fuschias, sedums and perovskia, or run up the lower stems of climbing roses.

The late-flowering group has been given the title 'Jackmanii' after the head of the dynasty, 'Jackmanii' (pictured on page 56). This hybrid was raised in 1858 as a cross between the viticella 'Atrorubens' and *C. lanuginosa*. Most of this group have *C. viticella* blood, which governs their late flowering, while *C. texensis* introduced red into a limited colour range of white, blue or purple. Do not be confused by other cultivars with the Jackman epithet, like 'Jackmanii Rubra' and 'Jackmanii Alba', which belong to the earlier large-flowered group. All late-flowering hybrids can be pruned hard, some almost to the ground, without any risk of losing flowers or injuring the plant (see page 141). Left unpruned, they will still flower but the old flowering stems will tend to die, leaving old, tangled and unsightly wood which is best removed, if only for aesthetic reasons.

The stars of this group are its dark purple forms – the eponymous 'Jackmanii', 'Jackmanii Superba' and the more recent 'Romantika', which was given a special award by the British Clematis Society. Unfortunately, together with another dark purple, 'Viola', all these clematis have a propensity for being infected with mildew, especially in dry weather (see page 147). But if they can be grown in an open position, with good air circulation around them, they may fare much better.

In recent years Uno Kivistik, from Estonia, was extremely prolific in breeding new cultivars of this group of clematis. He named a collection after an Estonian nursery rhyme – 'Entel', 'Tentel', 'Kommerei' and 'Trikatrei' – all of which are worth growing. Mikhail Orlov, from Kiev, raised 'Sputnik' and 'Negritianka'. These are easy and tough, similar in many ways to the viticellas, with their small flowers in colours ranging from the palest of pinks ('Entel') to the deepest purple ('Negritianka'). Bred in Japan, 'Teksa' and 'Iryuu' are both speckled like faded denim.

'Jackmanii Superba' AGM 1984
This hybrid is very close to 'Jackmanii' itself but differs in its broader sepals and the reddish tinge to its purple colouring. It is otherwise the same in both habit and flowering time. Thomas Cripps raised it from a cross between 'Jackmanii' and *C. lanuginosa* in 1880. Its beige anthers help to distinguish it from 'Gipsy Queen', which has red anthers, while those of 'Jackmanii' are creamy green.
HARD PRUNE

There are many dubious distinctions in the classification of these clematis. How can one separate 'Madame Julia Correvon' and 'M. Koster', both almost always listed as viticellas, from 'Prince Charles', Blue Angel or 'Victoria', which are classified here as part of the Jackmanii group? They all have medium-sized flowers that can be classified as neither large nor small, and thus fall into a no man's land between the two groups. Some plants simply refuse to be pigeon-holed easily. This is of no real consequence, as their treatment and cultivation are exactly the same.

Finally, I should mention the one that is always late for the party, 'Lady Betty Balfour'. Raised in 1910 by the Jackmans of Woking, she stubbornly refuses, by some genetic quirk, to flower until the very last minute, her deep violet-purple flowers sometimes not opening until autumn.

'Star of India' AGM 1993

Similar to, but livelier than, its parent 'Jackmanii', its dapper, well-dressed purple flowers are enhanced by a reddish bar, on a plant with less, but still sufficient, vigour. This is an old cultivar, raised by Thomas Cripps in 1867, from another cross between *C. lanuginosa* and 'Jackmanii'. The flower is often fuller, with more closely spaced sepals than shown here. One of the great contributions made by this clematis is in its role as the mother of the two texensis hybrids 'Duchess of Albany' and 'Sir Trevor Lawrence'. HARD PRUNE

'Prince Charles' (above)

This great all-round clematis has light blue to mauve-blue blooms with an exceptionally long flowering period during midsummer. It is one of the first of the late hybrids to open, and continues for a good six to eight weeks if the summer is not too hot. It is easily trained on supports or grown in mixed borders or containers. It was imported in the 1950s as an unnamed mystery hybrid by Alister Keay of New Zealand, who eventually gave it this name in 1975.

HARD PRUNE

Blue Angel (opposite)

Listed in Europe by its original Polish name 'Blekitny Aniol', this is one of the very best of the new generation of late clematis. Its relatively small (7.5–10cm), pale blue flowers have crimped edges and are beautifully textured. It shares this elegant puckered look with a pale pink Estonian variety called 'Entel'. Both have lightweight growth up to 3m, perfectly suited to trailing through mixed borders of small shrubs, roses and perennials. Raised by Brother Stefan Franczak, 1988.

HARD PRUNE

'Hagley Hybrid' AGM 1984 (right)
Often described as pink, 'Hagley Hybrid'
is actually tinged with a good bit of
mauve. It should therefore be kept away
from pure pink flowers, especially roses,
which would tend to make it look
slightly dirty, particularly as it fades.
Complemented by its dark red anthers, it
can seem more pink when planted with
blues and purples, especially when given
some shade. It is a profuse and reliable
performer for midsummer, growing to
2–3m. Raised by Percy Picton, 1945.
HARD PRUNE

'Comtesse de Bouchaud' AGM 1993
(opposite, below)
This is by far the most effective, reliable
and popular of the late large-flowered
pink clematis. Raised originally by
Francisque Morel around 1900, this is an
excellent plant for growing over arbours
or among shrubs. A slight caution, though,
about mixing it with roses: the pink is a
touch too mauve and may look dirty
among purer pink roses and could clash
with red ones. It is perhaps best grown
among purple- and blue-flowered shrubs
or in bronze- or silver-foliaged trees or
large shrubs, where it can reach to 4m.
HARD PRUNE

'Margaret Hunt' (above)

There is something oddly attractive about dusky mauve hybrids like this one and 'Hagley Hybrid' (opposite). They do not fight for attention but sit easily, without fuss, in mixed borders, simply adding colour and form in profusion without having to be dazzling. They fit in well among roses and mixed plantings of blue and white flowers. They are also very easy to grow, accommodating in size and can be pruned right down after flowering. The gappy flowers (10–15cm wide) are produced on a plant up to 4m tall.

HARD PRUNE

'Rhapsody'

Of all the blue hybrids in any group, 'Rhapsody' has the most exciting colour. Its deep inky indigo shade deepens with age, contrasting well with the cream stamens. It is a superb colour to brush among light pink roses, such as the climbing 'New Dawn' or Sharifa Asma. The flowers, 8–15cm across, appear on both old and new wood, so it could be light or hard pruned, growing to 3m. Two 'Rhapsodies' were introduced at about the same time but this version is almost certainly the one introduced by Barry Fretwell around 1995.
HARD PRUNE

'Gipsy Queen' AGM 1993

A cross between 'Jackmanii' and *C. patens* made by Thomas Cripps in 1877, 'Gipsy Queen' is one of the very best of the large-flowered hybrids for combining with other late summer-flowering plants such as roses, fuchsias or even dahlias. The deep violet-purple flowers are infused with a tinge of red that distinguishes it from 'Jackmanii Superba' (see page 98), whose flowers are exactly the same size and shape. It can climb up to 5m with long, searching growths that can be woven through shrubs or over perennials. Due to its *C. patens* blood, it can be light pruned for some earlier flowers but should generally be hard pruned. HARD PRUNE

'Rouge Cardinal'

What this plant lacks in strength of habit, it makes up for in intensity of colour and the harmony of its flowers, which are velvety crimson and well-rounded, the creamy filaments of the stamens tipped with dark red anthers. Grown without too much competition at the roots and fed well, it may reach 3m or more. The flowers, 10–15cm across, eventually fade to more of a purplish cerise. Raised in Orléans, France, by A. Girault, 1960s.

HARD PRUNE

'Ville de Lyon' AGM 1984

One of the first large-flowered hybrids to be successfully infused with the scarlet blood of *C. texensis*, 'Ville de Lyon' is strong growing, up to 4m, and very free flowering. Francisque Morel was a master in the use of this species, producing a peerless range of clematis that, 100 years later, even the most sophisticated breeder could not match. The flowers of 'Ville de Lyon' are unique in style and colour, opening to a bright crimson-red, quickly developing a paler centre to the quite rounded sepals. It is best given a partner to help disguise its lower stems which can become brown and unsightly.

HARD PRUNE

'Ernest Markham' AGM 1993

Ernest Markham was William Robinson's head gardener, and the two of them did much to promote clematis growing between the two world wars. Named in his honour, this cultivar was among a batch of seedlings given by Markham to Rowland Jackson, who introduced it in 1937. The woolly buds open into velvety crimson-to-magenta blooms, 10–15cm across, that fade to a subdued pinky red. Not always the easiest clematis to grow, it needs plenty of sunshine, like many red-flowered cultivars. If only light pruned, it will flower early but it reserves its best display for late summer. HARD PRUNE

'Madame Édouard André' AGM 1993

The star-shaped wine-red flowers, incurved
sepals and cream stamens are a perfect
complement to the soft form and colour of
white or pink roses. This hybrid, one of the
finest of the dark reds and crimsons, is
prolific but not too vigorous. It does best
in some sun. Raised in France by Baron
Veillard, pre-1893. (Also known in the
trade as America's Popular Red.)
HARD PRUNE

'Huldine' AGM 1984 (opposite, top left)

With its small (7.5–10cm), slightly cupped
flowers, 'Huldine' is occasionally listed among
the viticellas, though it has the appearance of
a large-flowered hybrid. Two clones exist, one
that is shy of flowering, the other boasting
beautiful pearly white blooms. Seen from
below, the flowers show a distinct mauve-pink
bar on the reverse. Quite vigorous, up to 5m,
it should be grown through large shrubs in a
sunny position. Part of a batch of plants given
by Francisque Morel to William Robinson, it
was introduced and given an Award of Merit
in 1934. HARD PRUNE

Wisley (above)

A modern-day Jackmanii type with some viticella blood, this clematis was raised by Ray Evison to commemorate the Royal Horticultural Society's bicentenary in 2004 and named after their garden in Surrey. Its mid-blue flowers, 10–12cm across, are typical of Jackmanii types, but with crinkled edges and cream stamens. Like others in this group, Wisley would look good among roses, and shows off well against variegated or silver foliage. It has the vigour and free-flowering habit of a viticella, growing to 2–3m. HARD PRUNE

'John Huxtable' (above)

A seedling of the peerless pink 'Comtesse de Bouchaud', found in the Devon garden of its namesake in the 1960s, this clematis is creamy white with cream stamens. The textured sepals, folding up at the edges, are slightly smaller (10–12cm) than most of the large-flowered hybrids. It is the closest we have yet come to a true white Jackmanii type. Although not as vigorous as the Comtesse, it can still reach 3–4m. It is best grown in some sun and looks beautiful among roses. HARD PRUNE

the viticellas

Native to southern Europe, from Italy eastwards to Greece and as far as Iran, *C. viticella* is the most important European species to be used in breeding. Cultivated in gardens since the sixteenth century, this species has also become naturalized in parts of central Europe where it grows in abandoned fields and over ruined buildings. It is a vigorous summer-flowering scrambler with four-sepalled purple-blue hanging bells. Further west, in Portugal, one sees a subspecies, *C. viticella* subsp. *campaniflora*, with smaller, pale mauve pendulous flowers, a delightful plant for naturalistic plantings.

This was the first group of clematis to get me truly hooked. The breeder and nurseryman John Treasure insisted in the 1970s that this tribe of clematis should be grown for their versatility in mixed plantings. At that time, low-maintenance gardens were all the rage, with carpets of heather and juniper for weed-free ground cover and winter colour. John planted his viticellas and texensis varieties through these otherwise rather flat and inert plantings to bring them to life in summer. Planted at the base of tall junipers, they can thrust 3m of growth upwards and outwards.

Viticellas and texensis varieties (see pages 114–17) are the perfect beginner's clematis because they are hardy, tough and can be hard pruned to the ground in late autumn or winter, while rarely suffering the indignities of clematis wilt. If proof were needed of the viticellas' endurance, it can be found in Barry Fretwell's discovery in 1981 of a double form which he called 'Mary Rose'. This actually turned out to be the same plant as one *C. viticella* 'Flore Pleno', mentioned by John Parkinson back in 1629. Another testament to their claim to posterity is that out of the 16 viticellas selected for this book, 13 were raised a century ago or more, over half of them bred by two French nurserymen, Morel and Lemoine.

Francisque Morel infused *C. viticella* with the then recently introduced scarlet *C. texensis* to produce a peerless new race of hybrids. He eventually gave up breeding clematis to concentrate on garden design, and handed over many of his hybrids to William Robinson. Ernest Markham, Robinson's head gardener, wrote in 1935 of his 'vivid memories of (Morel's) robust seedlings' which he planted at Gravetye in 1914, adding that 'these delightful varieties are still far too little known'. Among the new generation of viticellas, I see very few, if any, that could usurp the well-worn crowns of the likes of 'Kermesina', 'Royal Velours', 'Venosa Violacea' and 'Madame Julia Correvon'.

A small group of hybrids can trace their origins back to the pendulous 'Étoile Rose', one of Lemoine's hybrids from 1903, and have sometimes been listed as 'texensis' types. 'Pagoda', a pale mauve nodding flower, and its seedling,

the species
C. viticella, C. viticella subsp.
campaniflora

other species involved in the hybrids
*C. florida, C. hirsutissima,
C. integrifolia, C. lanuginosa,
C. patens, C. texensis*

'Black Prince' (right)

A genuinely dark, blackish claret-red that sustains its sombre mood throughout the flower's life. The widely spaced sepals and pendulous flowers, 6-9cm across, are close to *C. viticella* and so dark that they need a light background to be seen at all. Silver-foliaged trees and shrubs like *Pyrus salicifolia* 'Pendula' or *Elaeagnus angustifolia* would be strong enough to cope with its vigour (up to 4m). The odd trail could then be allowed to wander down through patches of herbaceous artemisia or anaphalis. Raised in New Zealand by Alister Keay, 1990. HARD PRUNE

'Abundance' (opposite)

This is a glorious cultivar, in terms of colour, size and vigour, the best for melding with shrubs. The warm, pinky red flowers, 5–8cm across, look wonderful alongside panicles of buddleia or as late-summer drapery slung over lilacs, philadelphus or any shrubs that are dull after flowering. Given some sun, it will flower well and grow to 4m or more. Francisque Morel raised this cultivar around 1900 and gave it to William Robinson, who introduced it through the Jackmans in 1937. Incredibly, it has never been given any award. HARD PRUNE

the darker amethyst-coloured 'John Treasure', were raised by John Treasure, while 'Odoriba', a pale pink version of 'Étoile Rose', comes from Japan. This small group, perhaps due a higher proportion of texensis blood, is a little more prone to mildew than the others. 'Black Prince', a truly dark purple, and the purple-blue 'Elvan' bear a much closer resemblance to *C. viticella* itself, while also inheriting its vigour and flower power.

The viticellas are ultra-hardy, and will grow in most soils that are neither too dry nor too wet. Although happy in shade, they tend to flower more profusely with more sun. As with all clematis, a good start can set them up for life. Viticellas do not always die right back to their crown. The tops of the main flowering stems tend to die in winter but new shoots can break out from old woody stems. Although they can be pruned hard to within 30cm of the ground, it is far better, especially when they are grown through tall shrubs, hedges and trees, just to cut them back in late winter or early spring, pruning back to well-placed buds that are facing in the direction you want them to travel. This will save a lot of training.

'M. Koster' (above)

This is a plant for informal settings, where it should be allowed to trail up to 4m at will, but not too low, as the mauve-pink to lilac-purple flowers are semi-nodding and would face the ground. The flowers are 10–14cm across and the sepals often roll and twist to create gaps between them. This is not generally seen as a good trait, but I think it adds to this hybrid's charming, lax mood. It is one of the earliest of the group to flower, continuing well into the summer. Raised by Koster, c.1890. HARD PRUNE

'Étoile Rose' AGM 1984 (right)

This exquisite nodding flower with its rich mix of red and satiny pinks, with paler tones on its reflexed sepals, hangs at the end of its stalk with perfect poise. In midsummer the profusion of flowers (5–8cm across) is carried on an open and enthusiastic plant, capable of reaching 4m. It is excellent and easy to grow through purple-, blue- or silver-foliaged shrubs but a little prone to mildew in some areas and in some seasons. It is the parent of three other fine clematis, 'Pagoda' (see page 31), 'Odoriba' and 'John Treasure', all of which have those same expressively shaped, recurved sepals. Raised in France by Victor Lemoine, *c.* 1903. HARD PRUNE

'Royal Velours' AGM 1993 (opposite)

This captivating variety has deep red-purple flowers with a satin-like sheen and green-black anthers. The sepals are rounded, recurving slightly. It is so dark that it not only needs a light background such as a white wall, or a silver- or gold-foliaged shrub, but it should also be placed where the sun can light it from behind. I know one magnificent specimen that grows 3–4m into the crown of a *Catalpa bignonioides* 'Aurea', the two plants setting each other off beautifully and lighting up magically in the moments just before a sunset. Raised by Morel, pre-1914, it won an Award of Merit in 1948. HARD PRUNE

'Venosa Violacea' AGM 1993   (above)
With quite a large flower for a viticella
(9–14cm across), possibly due to some
C. florida blood, this old cultivar is
essentially white and shot through with
violet–purple veins, hence its name. The
veins branch with increasing intensity
towards the edge, taking on more purple
as they go, so that the flower actually
looks more purple than white. It is less
vigorous than many in this group,
growing to only 3m, which makes it
suitable for a multitude of situations:
in borders, with roses or on obelisks.
Raised by Lemoine et Fils, 1883.
HARD PRUNE

'Minuet' AGM 1993 (left)

Nodding and flared, this distinct cultivar has deep pink-red margins around wide, white-feathered bars – conversely, it could be said to have white flowers with deeply veined red edges. Either way, it is a beautiful and lively flower, some blooms nodding, others facing out. Originally raised *c.*1900 by Francisque Morel, there are a few similar forms, all of them good, none of them better. 'Tango', 'Walenburg' and 'Cicciolina' all have varying amounts of colour displacement, while 'Little Nell' is altogether paler. HARD PRUNE

C. viticella 'Flore Pleno'
(opposite, below)

This pre-Linnaean name dates from the sixteenth century, around the time that Henry VIII's flagship, 'Mary Rose', was sunk (1545). The raising in 1982 of the old ship from the bottom of the Solent coincided with the revival of this old clematis after Barry Fretwell discovered it in a Devon garden. Its colour is a misty purple, much greyer and bluer than the other similarly shaped double, 'Purpurea Plena Elegans', which is dusky magenta (se page 45). A strong-growing plant to 4m or more. HARD PRUNE

the texensis group

Viorna is the botanical name given to this group of clematis species, most of them from south-eastern USA, but horticulturally they are better known by the group name of texensis, a broader church that includes all their closely related hybrids. *C. texensis* hails from the hill country (or Edwards Plateau) in central Texas, where it rambles in the mesquite, juniper and tall grasses, its flower colour varying from scarlet to pale maroon. The scarlet form, originally called *C. coccinea*, was introduced in 1868 to Europe, where it was – and continues to be – highly influential in the breeding of new varieties.

C. *viorna* itself was introduced from America in the eighteenth century, followed by *C. crispa*, the swamp clematis, and *C. pitcheri* in 1838. There were a few reported crosses made between them in Switzerland in the nineteenth century but these are probably extinct. All the viorna-type species have a characteristic urn-shaped flower, often with rather thick sepals, that in *C. viorna* itself are quite leathery. They are mostly small plants and quite intriguing. Their unusual flower shape, texture and colouring make them magnets for determined collectors and plantsmen. Some are challenging to grow but others, like *C. pitcheri* and *C. addisonii*, are fairly easy, given enough moisture and sun, in a well-drained loam. Many of the species are highly variable in colour, size and the shape of the flower. Along with the herbaceous group, this group of clematis is attracting much attention from serious breeders today, as it provides them with an astonishingly broad scope for creating new shapes and colours.

Three species first introduced to gardens over 150 years ago have at long last produced some worthy offspring. *C. crispa* was crossed in the USA with *C. viticella* to produce an exquisite pale lavender bell called 'Betty Corning'. *C. viorna* was also crossed with *C. viticella* in Estonia to create 'Kaiu', a vigorous plant with white bells tinted mauve. *C. pitcheri* has two new children, one from Barry Fretwell called 'Peveril Peach', and another from Mrs Kuriyama in Japan called 'Purple Treasure'.

All clematis in this group have one significant shortcoming: their susceptibility to mildew. Infections can completely disfigure the plant, flowers and all, and the only resort will be to spray with fungicides. Growing plants in an open position with good air circulation, or pruning down the first flush of growth to produce later, less vulnerable shoots may lessen that risk.

A special group of hybrids between *C. texensis* and the large-flowered hybrids was originally called the Wokingensis group. For many, these are

member species
C. crispa, C. fusca, C. integrifolia, C. texensis

lesser-known species
C. addisonii, C. coactilis, C. glaucophylla, C. hirsutissima, C. pitcheri, C. reticulata, C. versicolor, C. viorna

other species involved in the hybrids
C. lanuginosa, C. patens, C. viticella

'Princess Diana' (right)

Nothing but superlatives issue from the lips of anyone who has grown this brilliant hybrid raised by Barry Fretwell in 1984 from a cross between *C. texensis* and 'Bee's Jubilee'. Its luminous pink flowers may start opening in early summer, and continue into late summer. Cutting back old flowering shoots after the first main flush will encourage more of those later blooms. Less prone to mildew than others, it is excellent for border plantings, with roses or in a container. Originally called 'The Princess of Wales', it was renamed because a clematis existed with this name, a blue large-flowered hybrid that honoured the previous bearer of the title in 1875, the Danish wife of the future Edward VII. HARD PRUNE

'Sir Trevor Lawrence' (opposite)

In the 1890s, the Jackmans of Woking were very successful in their crossing of *C. texensis* with large-flowered hybrids like 'Star of India'. This hybrid was named after the President of the Royal Horticultural Society 1885–1913. Others in the series have been lost to cultivation. They all shared the unique 5–6cm long tulip shape, which opens to expose cream stamens. The colour is deep carmine to crimson, bluing with age, with a scarlet band at the centre of each sepal. It grows 1.5–3m in height. The similarly coloured 'Lady Bird Johnson' was raised by Barry Fretwell, by crossing *C. texensis* with 'Bee's Jubilee', the cross which also gave rise to 'Princess Diana' (above). HARD PRUNE

the most superlative of all clematis, their unique tulip-shaped flowers coming in rich shades of pink and deep red. Two of the original crosses were 'Duchess of Albany' and 'Sir Trevor Lawrence'. Results of later crosses include 'Gravetye Beauty', 'Lady Bird Johnson' and 'Princess Diana'. These can look wonderful trailing in shrubs such as the deciduous blue *Ceanothus* 'Gloire de Versailles' or cotoneasters, or just left to scramble in mixed borders.

This group is generally pruned hard to within 15cm of the ground, at any time during the winter.

C. crispa (left)

An American species from east and south USA, *C. crispa* is unaccountably rare in cultivation and should be more widely sought out. It is a fine example of the grace and refinement shared by others in this group. Many species in the texensis group are highly variable, and *C. crispa* is no exception. This outstanding form was growing in Mrs Kuriyama's collection at the back of a Buddhist temple in Japan. HARD PRUNE

C. addisonii (opposite)

The urn-shaped flower is typical of so many of the viorna-type species found in North America, including *C. viorna* itself, to which the flower of this species bears a close resemblance. The colour is variable, from pale rosy mauve to dark, rich rosy purple, but always with a creamy white interior. It forms a small scrambling and non-climbing plant, up to 40cm high, which, although herbaceous in nature, may form a woody base. Native to Virginia and South Carolina, it is hardy down to -20°C, but needs a warm position with good drainage in winter. HARD PRUNE

late-flowering species

The connection between members of this group lies in their small flowers that open in summer or autumn. Among this band of strays that do not conveniently fit into the other late-flowering groups are some of the most beautiful and fragrant of the species, many being most suitable for draping through trees, hedges and other more naturalistic settings.

The two American species *C. virginiana* and *C. ligusticifolia*, like their close relative *C. vitalba* (old man's beard or traveller's joy), are too vigorous for most gardens. *C. virginiana*, known rather sinisterly in the USA as 'the devil's darning needle', has given rise to the herbaceous scrambler 'Mrs Robert Brydon' (see page 131), through a cross with *C. heracleifolia*. 'Grace', a hybrid between *C. ligusticifolia* and *C. serratifolia* raised by Frank Skinner in Canada in 1925, is a lovely late-flowering hardy climber with cream flowers and prominent wine-red stamens that is best planted in full sun to flower and grow well.

C. vitalba could be grown in a wild garden. If pruned hard each year, and with its roots restricted by the competition of tree or old hedge roots, it may grow no more than 3m each year. When hard pruned, it will flower later than those in the wild, but the flowers may not set in enough time before the frosts to produce those wonderful seedheads. Its Asian cousins, *C. grata* and *C. brevicaudata*, although not often seen outside serious collections, are worth considering for trailing into old trees, over old tree stumps or on walls.
C. potaninii grows in the deep wooded valleys of south-western China, where it graces natural shrubberies with its pure white blooms and finely cut foliage. *C. flammula* is found all over the Mediterranean rim where its scrambles over the scrub, often in quite arid conditions. A good form of it will grow 3m in a garden, its clouds of white flowers filling the air with a musty sweetness. It has passed this fragrance on to its offspring *C. × aromatica* (see page 125) and *C. × triternata* 'Rubromarginata'. Its oriental cousin, *C. terniflora*, has a similar fragrance and is esteemed on the eastern seaboard of the USA where it has become naturalized. Also scented is *C. rehderiana*, a wonderful plant for the late-summer garden with its clusters of primrose bells, though on a cold day in early autumn the scent may be somewhat less noticeable. *C. connata* is a similar but rangier plant with no fragrance at all, but it is well worth growing nonetheless.

the species
Europe: *C. flammula, C. vitalba*
Asia: *C. aethusifolia,*
C. brevicaudata, C. connata,
C. grata, C. potaninii,
C. rehderiana, C. terniflora,
C. trichotoma
North America: *C. ligusticifolia,*
C. virginiana

C. x *triternata* 'Rubromarginata'

A tricky name for a wonderful plant.
A hybrid between *C. viticella* 'Rubra' and
C. flammula, raised in England in the
1860s, it concentrates all the best
attributes of both parents. With the
vigour, hardiness and pinky purple colour
of the viticella, and the delicious fragrance
and starriness of *C. flammula*, it is a lovely
plant for an open, sunny site or to grow
against a wall, where the heat can draw
out its hawthorn scent. In shady places it
will tend to become rather weak, thin and
a little bit dingy. It reaches 3–4m and can
develop into quite a cascade of colour and
fragrance. HARD PRUNE

C. *terniflora* (opposite)

This robust species originates from China,
Korea and Japan, where it grows in
woodland margins and on roadsides. In its
adopted home on the eastern seaboard of
the USA (where it is known incorrectly
as *C. paniculata*, a name that belongs to a
New Zealand species), it has found much
the same habitats and is considered almost
a native. Known also as the autumn
clematis, it may not, in certain climates,
flower in time to beat the first frosts.
The form 'Robusta' has larger leaves
highlighted with silvery veins.
HARD PRUNE

A real collectable and a delightful small climber is *C. aethusifolia*, the so-called parsley-leaved clematis. Its finely dissected leaves are pale green, a perfect foil for the tiny creamy yellow bells that lightly sprinkle the plant in late summer. Introduced in France in 1861, *C. aethusifolia* comes from China, where it can be seen on rocky slopes near the Great Wall. It is rare not because of any problems with cultivation but due to the unfortunate and stubborn reluctance of new plants to be raised from cuttings or seeds.

All clematis in this group can be hard pruned.

C. potaninii (above)

Introduced in 1911, *C. potaninii* (sometimes known as *C. fargesii* var. *souliei*) was named after a Russian explorer who originally discovered it in western China in 1885. Growing vigorously to 5m, with attractive serrated leaves, it carries white flowers with prominent yellow stamens in singles or groups of two or three. It is one of the easiest and most attractive of the midsummer-flowering species, blooming earlier if left unpruned. The subspecies *C. potaninii* subsp. *fargesii* is less vigorous but also less floriferous. HARD PRUNE

C. viticella subsp. *campaniflora* (left)
Native to Portugal, this is a paler and smaller version of *C. viticella*. The small 2–3cm, pale mauve open bells are produced in midsummer on a vigorous plant growing to 4m. It could be grown into dark conifers, *Salix exigua*, or even purple-leaved shrubs. A hybrid with *C. viticella*, called 'Lisboa', has larger and darker blue flowers. HARD PRUNE

C. rehderiana AGM 1993
(opposite, below)
This clematis was formerly called *C. nutans*, meaning nodding, because of its pendulous clusters of small, soft yellow flowers that are borne in late summer against a background of hairy nettle-like leaves. The best forms carry a sweet fragrance, especially on warm evenings. Young plants take a while to settle down and will need plenty of room, reaching to 8m in fertile soils, which makes it suited to romping around informal shrubberies or on the sunny sides of hedges. It might overwhelm many wall shrubs like ceanothus, but the purple smoke bush (*Cotinus*) will make a good foil for the pale flowers. Introduced from western China by Père Aubert in 1898, and again by E. H. Wilson in 1908. Given an Award of Merit in 1936.
HARD PRUNE

the orientalis group

Bright yellow lantern-shaped flowers and fabulous silvery seedheads are the two outstanding features of this group's most popular members. The species belong to the subgenus *Meclatis*, but the group as a whole is known as the orientalis group (occasionally also described as the tangutica group). For a long time, one of the most popular forms was *C. orientalis* 'Orange Peel', an allusion less to the colour, which is more like grapefruit, but to the thick, puckered texture of the sepals. This plant, with its slender glaucous foliage, has now been more correctly identified as *C. tibetana* subsp. *vernayi* 'Orange Peel', a plant collected by Ludlow, Sherriff and Elliot in Tibet in 1947; it is still generally known as 'Orange Peel', however. The true *C. orientalis* is a small-flowered plant with brick-orange and yellow flowers.

The other major player is *C. tangutica*, similar in many ways to *C. tibetana* subsp. *vernayi*, but with more open lanterns and greener foliage. This species also grows in Tibet and China, where Christopher Brickell, following in the footsteps of the great plant collectors Reginald Farrer and William Purdom, saw it growing near Lake Koko Nor. It was forming mounds so wide and high that he could not 'recall ever seeing it as a climber even when shrubs or trees were close by'. The best forms of *C. tangutica* are 'Lambton Park' and 'Bill MacKenzie'; the latter has rounder, firmer sepals inherited from *C. tibetana*. All are easily grown in full sun, even in quite poor, dry soils. I would love to see these clematis grown as they often are in the wild, in wide open spaces, with ornamental grasses, gravel, boulders and a few gnarled trees. Maintenance might be a bit tricky but the effect could be astounding. It is worth seeking out the true forms of the best of this group because seedlings, which can pop up self-sown in the garden, are often inferior and may take years to flower.

Like the viticellas, the orientalis types carry a mat of old flowering stems which might need to be tidied with a pair of hedging shears after the seedheads have gone past their best, in the new year. Any further pruning can be done as the new shoots emerge in early spring, cutting just above the most vigorous of them. Even with this treatment, after a few years the whole plant can become a dense, scrappy tangle, demanding more drastic treatment. This can be done by cutting the plant down to within 30cm of the ground in spring, with no detriment to the plant and no reduction in flower production, except a delay of two or three weeks in the start of flowering.

the species
C. akebioides, C. intricata, C. ladakhiana, C. serratifolia, C. tangutica, C. tibetana subsp. *vernayi*

'Bill MacKenzie' AGM 1993 (left)
This beautiful hybrid has a profuse display of flowers and silver seedheads. If trimmed back lightly, it flowers from early summer to autumn. Hard-pruned plants start flowering later but continue for longer. HARD PRUNE

'Lambton Park' (below)
This clear yellow form of *C. tangutica* was discovered by Tom Bennett in Lambton Park, Co. Durham, U.K. It has some of the largest flowers in the group, with a long-lasting mass of seedheads. HARD PRUNE

'Anita' (above)

Hybrids between this group and others were unheard of until the unexpected arrival of this child of *C. potaninii* and *C. tangutica*. Dubbed the white tangutica (all orientalis species are some shade of yellow), 'Anita' represents an intermediate between its parents, being vigorous to 5m with open, pendulous white flowers in summer. Best in some sun. Raised in Holland by Rinus, 1988. HARD PRUNE

'My Angel' (right)

This hybrid is intriguing in its brick-orange and yellow colour and the shape of its flowers, whose sepals curl up at the edges. The seedheads are produced in a dense mass. It is a vigorous, often suckering plant for full sun, where it is reasonably drought-tolerant. Raised in Holland 1997 by Wim Snoeijer, from a cross between *C. intricata* and the true *C. orientalis*. HARD PRUNE

herbaceous clematis

Unlike other clematis, those in the herbaceous group do not possess twining leaf petioles. This excellent and diverse group is not as widely grown as it deserves to be. This may be partly due to the fact that they do not look their best in a sales pot and that, excepting some of the tubulosa group, their uncertain floppy habit makes them baffling to place in the garden. Once you have mastered their needs, however, there is as much satisfaction in growing these as the other groups.

All herbaceous forms are hardy and easy to grow in any reasonable soil, in sun or part shade, and they suffer from very few ailments. They should be hard pruned at any time during the winter months.

THE INTEGRIFOLIAS

C. integrifolia hails from central Europe into Asia, where it grows in bushy places, meadows and riversides. It has twisted blue sepals on a short clump-forming plant which, if grown in fertile soil in the open, spreads itself out in a circle, leaving a flattened, often leafless centre. The tips of the shoots then lift up to produce a good succession of summer-borne flowers followed by beautiful seedheads. If placed in a border, this flattened look can be uncomfortable for those seeking order. To make them look their best, I plant integrifolias at the top of low retaining walls, on banks, under rocks or in borders tucked under the outer skirts of shrubs and roses.

Once established they require little attention. A bunch of twigs or pea-sticks could be stuck into the ground around the crowns in spring, to provide *C. integrifolia* with a support where it reaches up to 1m. This same treatment would be ideal for those grown in pots but they can look strangled and rather awkward if pulled up in a bunch around a single cane.

C. integrifolia has a number of coloured forms as well as its more natural blue, ranging from white to deep pink. Two new ones from Japan, 'Hakurei', with white sepals tinged in blue, and 'Hanujima', deep pink, are more dwarf, growing only to 50cm. *C. integrifolia* grows readily from seed, and growers sometimes release inferior forms into commerce. One of the victims of this is *C. integrifolia* 'Rosea', usually a fine rosy pink which can be offered up as a washed-out mauve-pink. They are fairly easy to propagate from cuttings.

Integrifolias are easy to grow, extremely hardy (the species is even naturalized in Ontario, Canada), and flower better with some sun. Like all herbaceous plants, their growth dies down to the crown each year. The old growth can be pruned away at any time during the winter months, after the attractive seedheads have lost their sheen.

the species
C. heracleifolia, C. hirsutissima, C. integrifolia, C. recta, C. stans, C. tubulosa

other species involved in the hybrids
C. flammula, C. lanuginosa, C. patens, C. viticella

C. x aromatica (right)

An early hybrid, probably raised in France prior to 1855, from a cross between *C. integrifolia* and *C. flammula*. It has the best from each parent: from *C. integrifolia* a dwarf herbaceous habit and dark blue flowers, and from *C. flammula* its outward-facing, star-like shape, contrasting boss of cream stamens and lovely fragrance. A sprawling mound of up to 1.5m, it can be grown on a frame or through a grey-leaved shrub to show off its dark flowers. Like *C. flammula*, it is best grown in full sun in well-drained soil to encourage compact growth, more flower and an intense fragrance. HARD PRUNE

C. integrifolia 'Alba' (opposite)

C. integrifolia is a striking blue species native to central Europe. It sends shoots up to 1m that fall down and rise again, carrying their twisted pendulous flowers at the tips. Colour variations have been selected from white through to light pink, and from deep pink to all shades of blue. The flowers are followed by silky seedheads. This great all-round plant has sired and mothered hundreds of hybrids. HARD PRUNE

'Fascination' (right)

A typically modern hybrid with *C. fusca* var. *violacea* as one parent and *C. x diversifolia* as the other, creating a short, compact plant to 1.5m. It has dusky violet-purple flowers with thick fleshy sepals, 2–3cm across, followed by attractive seedheads. This plant fits modern tastes: small in size, intriguing flowers, a long season of interest and good-looking in a pot. One for the cognoscenti. Raised in Holland by Wim Snoeijer, 1990s. HARD PRUNE

Petit Faucon (above)

Meaning little falcon, but with a flower more like a butterfly, the glossy, deep violet-blue flowers of this hybrid are scattered lightly over 1.5m stems. The colour contrasts with the creamy yellow stamens, while the young foliage is bronze-tinted. A chance seedling from 'Daniel Deronda', sired most probably by *C. integrifolia*, it was raised by Raymond Evison in the 1980s and registered as 'Evisix'. An equally good garden plant, but not quite as dark, is 'Rising Star', from Japan. HARD PRUNE

THE DIVERSIFOLIA GROUP

A number of hybrids have been raised between *C. integrifolia* and *C. viticella*, their names occasionally prefixed by × *diversifolia*. These include what may have been the first-ever hybrid raised, *C.* × *eriostemon*, in the 1830s. Their habit combines the herbaceous nature of *C. integrifolia* with the vigour of *C. viticella*, producing long, non-climbing shoots that are lanky and gaunt, their flowers appearing at a height of 1–3m. Given a suitable support of twigs or wires, however, you would barely know that this group had lost the ability to climb. Shrub roses, hydrangeas, viburnums and philadelphus all make perfect hosts, the clematis flowers often popping up in summer out of the top of the shrubs.

As this group becomes better understood, the demand for new forms is increasing. We can expect a lot more variations on this theme in the coming years, especially in crosses with the texensis group.

C. × *durandii* AGM 1993

(opposite, right)

The indigo-blue flowers of *C.* × *durandii* complement yellow flowers and golden foliage in a border. This is an admirable border plant, the downy and almost shrubby growth of up to 2m being rather stiff but not too dense. Raised in Lyon, France, by the Durand brothers, pre-1870. HARD PRUNE

C. × *diversifolia* 'Heather Herschell'

(right)

In recent years a few breeders have focused on raising pink versions of *C.* × *durandii* and *C.* × *diversifolia*. This pink diversifolia was raised by Barry Fretwell in 1999, just before Wim Snoeijer in Holland introduced his duo of 'Hendryetta', with a suggestion of the integrifolia twist, and Inspiration, his version of a pink durandii. Easy to grow, they bear nodding flowers on plants up to 2m tall which would be perfect for wandering around the papery domes and cones of hydrangeas. HARD PRUNE

Blue Rain

This is a translation from its original Russian name of 'Sinee Dozhd'. Raised by Professor Beskaravainaya in the Ukraine in 1979, it is similar to *C.* × *diversifolia* but, in my experience, a distinct improvement. A profusion of larger, deep violet-blue flowers, 4–6cm across, are produced over a longer season. I have grown it up the outer branches of a lilac, the flowers raining out at head height. It grows to 1.5–2.5m. HARD PRUNE

Harlow Carr

Introduced to celebrate the bicentenary of the Royal Horticultural Society in 2004, and named after their garden in Harrogate, Yorkshire, this variety was raised by Ray Evison. With four deep purple-blue sepals, on flowers 7–10cm across, with blackish brown anthers, he must have been thinking along the same lines as Masatake Udagawa in Japan, who had crossed *C. integrifolia* with *C. florida* to produce the almost identical 'Aphrodite' in 1995. Their four sepals, colour and inability to climb would both have been inherited from *C. integrifolia*, while their dark purple stamens and extensive flowering come from *C. florida*. Both are excellent subjects for mixed plantings and container growing. HARD PRUNE

'Alionushka' AGM 2002

Raised at the Ukraine's State Nikitsky
Botanic Gardens by A. N. Volosenko-Valenis
and M. A. Beskaravainaja, 1961, by crossing
C. integrifolia with 'Nezhdannyi'. It inherits
the former's herbaceous habit, reaching up
to 3m but, being unable to twine, needs the
support of other plants or regular tying in
on trellis. The deep pink flowers, fading
slightly at the edges, appear high up on the
plant. The attractive twisting sepals are
characteristic of *C. integrifolia*. HARD PRUNE

THE TUBULOSAS OR HERACLEIFOLIAS

C. tubulosa and *C. heracleifolia* look the least like what most people would
recognize as a clematis, neither sprawling nor climbing, but growing into a self-
supporting clump (see pages 130–31). They have bold vine-like leaves on stems
growing from a more or less woody base. In late summer, tall flowering shoots
emerge above the foliage, presenting whorls and clusters of small tubular flowers,
some deliciously scented, in shades of violet-blue. Their foliage is handsome, the
kind that associates well with other marginal woodlanders that enjoy moist
fertile soils, like Japanese anemones, astilbes and hostas. In mixed flower borders
they make good companions for late-flowering crocosmias and heleniums. As
they turn yellow-brown in autumn, the leaves take on a mysterious aroma that is
best compared to a cross between marzipan and a sweet Dutch pipe tobacco.

C. tubulosa 'Wyevale' AGM 1993 (above)
For much of the year this form of herbaceous
C. tubulosa, with larger flowers than the type,
makes healthy, ground-covering clumps of
bold, coarse foliage before sending up flower
spikes in mid- to late summer. It will associate
well with other border perennials that need
a lot of room to expand such as heleniums,
rudbeckias or geraniums. HARD PRUNE

'Praecox' AGM 1993 (opposite)
This is one of the few garden plants with
C. vitalba blood. The cross between
C. tubulosa and *C. × jouiniana* produced a
sprawling, woody herbaceous plant whose
annual growth covers 3–4m. It is a plant for
the edge of the wilderness or to surge into
tough shrubs, rambler roses or small trees.
Its flower clusters are produced six weeks
earlier than *C. × jouiniana*. Raised in France
by Simon Louis Frères, *c*.1900. HARD PRUNE

'Mrs Robert Brydon' (right)

Christopher Lloyd is unabashedly damning about this clematis, calling it 'a poor thing', but I must trot to its defence, having used it in America and England in large mixed borders with buddlejas and to cover areas of spent spring bulbs. The flowers, in their off-white to pale mauve sprays, are easily shamed by bright border plants. But foaming in hedges and around wild roses, their modesty is most welcome. From a cross between *C. tubulosa* and *C. virginiana*, it resembles a smaller version of *C.* × *jouiniana*, growing to only 2.5m. Raised in Ohio, USA, by Robert Brydon, 1935. HARD PRUNE

good practice

Most clematis can be easily grown without too much care beyond watering and feeding. Even their pruning is quite straightforward, provided a few basic principles have been grasped. If you wish to multiply your clematis, they are also very obliging, offering several means to propagate them, from raising the odd plant through layering to the exciting prospect of growing a new variety from seed. Once established, many clematis can thrive for years without special pampering and with no additional nutrition other than that which a moisture-retentive, fertile soil will naturally provide. That said, given a little knowledge and a degree of tender loving care, clematis will respond in kind and reward the gardener with years of pleasure.

'Blue Boy' (left), a paler blue version of the herbaceous C. × diversifolia, *was raised in Canada in 1947.* Rosa rugosa *is the ideal host for height, support and complementary late-summer flowering.*

planting

BUYING PLANTS

The best source for buying clematis is a reputable specialist nursery, who will be able to advise you on cultivation and ensure that a plant is correctly named. Most such nurseries (see addresses, page 156) sell a wide range of varieties, usually in 2-litre, but occasionally 3-litre, pots; many offer a mail-order service.

Nurseries that offer 3-litre pots do so mainly to serve the garden-centre retail trade, which needs plants to look good on the display benches for a long season, rather than having to re-stock continually with fresh plants. Some garden centres may even sell clematis in 5-litre pots – perhaps even bigger. Unless you are desperate for immediate impact, these larger pots are unnecessary and you will gain little in the long term. As I have learned from experience, there may be a negative impact even in the short term. It isn't uncommon to see large plants actually shrink in their first season, while a well-grown 2-litre plant, placed into well-prepared soil early in the year, should romp away, sometimes covering several metres in one season. However, 3-litre pots are entirely appropriate for vigorous clematis like *C. montana* and the orientalis group that can quickly outgrow smaller pots.

The number of canes in a pot is mostly irrelevant, if not rather deceptive. A plant in full flower spiralling around three canes might in fact have only one very long, thin shoot. A clematis grown on a single cane, with no flowers but with a number of stronger shoots that have not even reached the top of the cane, will make a far better plant. When you buy from a good mail-order company the young plant may have been chopped back – this can often be beneficial.

The cheap and cheerful smaller plants offered in 9cm pots at bulk discount, or sold at markets and flower shows, should come with a warning. Planting them out in the garden straight away is risky. They should really be pampered in their first year by potting them on into a 2- or 3-litre container, ready to plant out once the roots have filled out the compost. Newspapers and magazines often make special offers in which they are not required to specify the size of plant. These offers are not necessarily cheaper; indeed, you may see 9cm or 1-litre pots offered at the same or a higher price than 2-litre plants sold through mail order.

Although container stock is designed to be sold at any time of year, there is an optimum time to buy. I like to plant clematis in mid-spring when the soil is just beginning to warm up, and the full growing season lies ahead. Nurseries often have their freshest and liveliest stock at this time of year. However, a good plant can be planted at almost any time of year, especially if you are able to water well, and autumn is an equally suitable time for hardy clematis.

CHOOSING GOOD

A sturdy plant should have three or four stout shoots. A plant that has been recently cut down, showing no flowers, may well be a better buy than a thin plant in full flower.

Ask to examine the rootball when you buy a clematis at a nursery or garden centre. A good plant should produce a potful of fleshy roots that may spiral round the pot once.

QUALITY PLANTS

A weak plant with only one or two thin shoots may support a few tempting flowers, but will grow away weakly. In this case, cut the plant down to 10cm before planting, to promote some vigour.

The roots of some species, like this C. alpina, are fine and fibrous, in contrast to the white fleshy roots displayed by the majority of clematis.

WHAT TO LOOK FOR

Try not to fall for a pretty face. A plant that has some handsome flowers on it does not necessarily mean it is the best of the bunch. Look for a plant with more than one stem, preferably three or four, which should be stout and vigorous. In the absence of flowers, look carefully at the label; most labels are fairly true to the colour and shape of the flower and often contain useful information.

It is not usually necessary to tease out the roots of pot-grown clematis as their dense, fleshy roots do not constrain themselves too much. Some of the best varieties of clematis, however, do not make good-looking retail plants and many of the orientalis group are so vigorous that they soon feel the limitations of their pots and start to look past their best. But, even if they are rather root-bound, these clematis will usually still grow away to make grand specimens. A plant that is severely pot-bound should, of course, be avoided altogether.

PLANTING OUT

Clematis are fairly catholic in their taste for soils, but in general they prefer a moisture-retentive loam. Their least favourite soils are those that are very acid, dry or sandy. It is often recommended that garden clematis be planted in a shady spot with stones placed over their roots. This may help to retain moisture but it is also the perfect environment for slugs, snails and earwigs, sworn enemies of clematis. It is better to plant them in a more open position and cover their roots with sharp grit or manure to protect them from both heat and pests. Give them plenty of water, especially in the first two or three years while they are establishing. Provided with a good start in life and a modicum of aftercare, they should reward the gardener with years of delight.

Most clematis need to be planted deeper than usual, as a precaution against wilt. Planting susceptible clematis with 7.5–10cm of the plant's stems and a few buds buried below soil level means that the plant has a chance of surviving an attack of wilt (see page 146). The plant may still appear to have been killed off, but only as far as ground level, the buried buds remaining unaffected and free to regenerate the plant. This practice is unnecessary for many small-flowered and species clematis that are not prone to wilt; indeed, in very heavy soils, plants buried too deep may suffer unduly.

Some authorities suggest that young clematis should be pruned back before planting, however this will vary from plant to plant. Pruning back will stimulate vigorous new growth and greatly benefit a plant with, for example, a single thin shoot. If the plant already has good strong shoots, there will be no need to prune it back, though trimming off any thin, weedy growth is always a good idea.

Water the clematis in its container an hour or two before planting. Plant a clematis as you would any new shrub or rose, digging a large hole up to 45cm wide and deep. Mix the removed soil with some rotted manure and bonemeal, then replace some of this loosened soil in the bottom of the hole. Check the soil level and make allowances for burying the stem by about 8cm if necessary.

PLANTING BY A WALL

If planting a clematis to grow against a house or garden wall, be aware of how dry the base of a wall can be and plant up to 30cm away. Under the overhanging eaves of a house, the soil can become dry, powdery and devoid of texture. If this is the case, plant the clematis far enough away from the wall for the rain to reach it, and train it back towards the wall with canes and wires. Bear in mind that old dry stone walls can be perfect hiding places for mice and snails.

PLANTING TO GROW INTO A TREE

To grow clematis through a tree or large shrub, bear in mind that some trees and shrubs are more-clematis friendly than others. Trees like beech and shrubs like viburnums possess dense root systems that lie close to the surface, making the

AGAINST A WALL

1 *After digging the hole, place the plant, still in its pot, in the hole to check that the depth is correct. The top of the pot should be 7.5–10cm below soil level. The hole should be at least twice as wide as the pot.*

2 *Remove the plant, inverting the pot and easing the rootball out by tapping the edge of the pot or gently squeezing the sides. Do not pull it out by the cane! Slide the pot off, discard it and, holding the base of the rootball, turn the plant the right way up and gently lower it into the hole.*

3 *After planting, refill the hole with good soil, mixed well with some well-rotted manure. Gently firm it around the roots, then give the whole plant a thoroughly good soaking. Topdress with a mulch of well-rotted manure or grit (see Feeding and watering, page 144).*

4 *Untie the plant from its cane(s) and spread out the shoots to train against the wall, using more canes if necessary to help it on its way.*

1 If the clematis is to live in a pot for a few years, choose one at least 45cm deep and 40cm wide. Cover the drainage holes with crocks, then fill with a gritty, loamy compost.

2 After planting, top up with more compost. The level should be 2–4cm below the rim of the pot to allow for watering.

3 Clematis grown in containers will need some support, like this wigwam made of woven hazel.

establishment of a new clematis more difficult. Plant the clematis well away from the base of the host plant, preferably well outside the 'drip line', or the edge of its crown.

PLANTING IN A BORDER

If planting clematis in a border, choose the neighbours carefully. Some herbaceous plants, like asters and alchemilla, and many ground covers, such as ivy, have voracious and greedy root systems which can soon stifle a clematis. Choose more generous neighbours, like roses, iris, sedums or salvias, whose root systems will not compete unfairly with the clematis roots. Better still, allow the clematis an area of 50cm diameter free of any competition. A well-prepared new border will give a clematis the best chance to get established before having to deal with the encroachment of its host's roots and its dense canopy. Vigorous clematis like *C. montana* and the orientalis types will have little trouble, but many of the large-flowered hybrids will gradually fade away over a number of years without proper attention.

When planting into a tree, plant well away from the trunk so that the clematis is able to find its own source of food and water. The clematis will soon work its way into the host plant by following a cane or guy wire running up into it from the ground.

PLANTING IN A CONTAINER

Choose a pot of a suitable size (see Growing in containers, page 60) and follow the instructions for planting clematis in the ground, burying the stems of wilt-susceptible large-flowered hybrids by 5–10cm. The potting compost should always contain some loam: an excellent mixture is made up of one part light multi-purpose compost and one part John Innes No. 2, as these contain slow-release fertilizers. Clematis in pots will need artificial supports such as canes or twigs, bound together with wires or string, or you can use a ready-made support. Bear in mind that plants growing in containers are much more vulnerable to vine weevil attack than those planted in the ground (see page 147).

pruning

The subject of pruning clematis has an undeserved reputation for being obscure. In fact, once a few basic principles have been assimilated, it is straightforward. First you need an understanding of the classification into three groups:

Group One (no pruning) This group of winter- and spring-flowering clematis requires little or no pruning, except for when a plant needs renewal.

Group Two (light pruning) This group of early-flowering large hybrids is best given a light prune in late winter, removing some old shoots to retain a number of strong stems.

Group Three (hard pruning) All the late summer-flowering clematis can be pruned hard, without any risk of losing flowers or injuring the plant.

GROUP ONE

The 'no prune' regime applies to all the early-flowering clematis, including the atragenes (alpinas and macropetalas), the montanas and the evergreen clematis (*C. armandii, C. cirrhosa* and the New Zealanders). While they require no regular pruning, if after a few years they form an unsightly mass of tangled twigs, they

PRUNING GROUP ONE

1 *Most Group One clematis are spring flowering and need no regular pruning. If the plant becomes overgrown, as here, and some pruning is required, carry this out immediately after flowering.*

2 *The pruning can be quite severe if necessary, but on* C. montana *always retain some younger shoots as the older, thicker shoots may simply not regenerate.*

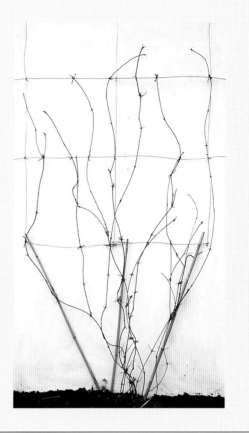

Group Two clematis can often become an ugly mesh of old stems and dead flower heads (right). Take the plant off the wires and remove old stems and thin shoots, leaving a selection of healthy, vigorous stems. Shorten these by a quarter to one-third, then replace on the wires (far right).

Although you can prune at any time in winter, it is easier to see the best places to cut when the new buds are emerging in late winter to early spring (above).

could benefit from having their old and weak growth cut out immediately after flowering. As most of this group flower very early in the year, they will have the whole summer ahead to make new growth and will produce flowers again the following year.

Severe pruning is fine for *C. cirrhosa* and *C. armandii* and the atragenes can also be pruned very hard, though older plants may take a year or two to recover. Some caution should be exercised with *C. montana*, however. This clematis can get out of control in confined places and drastic action may need to be taken by cutting the plant right back. In most cases it will shoot again, but very old plants may be reluctant to regenerate. I would recommend cutting a very old plant back in stages over a period of two or three years, leaving some of the thinner, younger shoots progressively to take over the reins.

GROUP TWO

The 'light prune' group includes all the early large-flowered hybrids and their double and semi-double forms. Although known also as the 'optional' group, the early large-flowered hybrids will always benefit from some pruning to give of their best. Left alone and unpruned, they will bear smaller flowers and eventually carry too much dead growth muddled in with the new. Pruning can take place at any time from late autumn to late winter.

We should think of these plants as needing a well-balanced framework of half a dozen or more good stems. The rest of the growth, including old cracked stems and persistent dead leaves, should all be removed. The tops of the selected stems can be shortened down to the highest (1.5–2.5m above ground) and strongest-looking buds. These buds, conditioned in the previous season, will produce shoots that carry an early crop of large flowers. Pruning in late winter or early spring, as the new buds are swelling, makes it much easier to judge which are the strongest. The best of these will be plump and borne in pairs.

The large-flowered hybrid clematis planted on the left has been pruned at the same time as the climbing rose, in late winter. They will need pruning this hard only once every three to four years to remove all old woody growth. The lighter the pruning, the earlier the flowers will appear, while pruning a bit harder will delay and prolong the flowering of both climbers.

At temperatures below –18°C, flower buds and even entire stems may be killed or damaged, but not the entire plant. This will have the same effect on the clematis as if it had been hard pruned and there will then be a later crop of smaller flowers. In those climates where temperatures regularly dive below –18°C, give winter protection by covering the crowns of large-flowered hybrids with soil or brushwood. It would also be best to choose hybrids that more reliably produce a good crop of flowers late in the year (see page 154). You could then treat these more like a late-flowering hybrid (see Group Three, opposite). Varieties like 'Niobe', 'Ernest Markham' and 'William Kennett', members of Group Two, are close in habit to the clematis belonging to Group Three so one can, with care, get the best of both worlds: a mixture of light and hard pruning will produce a light early crop, followed by a good late showing of flowers.

Some authorities have tried to make finer distinctions within this group of clematis, attributing their ability to flower later to the amount of 'lanuginosa' or 'viticella' blood in them, or their inability to repeat flower to their 'patens' blood. In truth, the mixed parentage of many of these hybrids makes this all rather speculative. Observation and experience are a far better key to success.

Most double large-flowered clematis will produce double flowers only in their first, early-summer flush. The second crop, if it materializes at all, is almost always single-flowered. Arctic Queen and 'Multi Blue' are among the few exceptions to this rule. Generally, these double-flowered cultivars would not be suitable for very cold areas where the buds may be damaged, distorted or destroyed by hard and late frosts.

1 *Group Three clematis can be hard pruned from autumn to late winter. Autumn may be preferred if you wish to tidy up the garden. Here a herbaceous clematis has been flowering in a hydrangea.*

2 *Prune the clematis down to within 10cm of the ground. If you leave this until late in winter, new shoots may already be breaking out, in which case you should prune to just above the strongest of these.*

GROUP THREE

The 'hard prune' regime applies to late-flowering hybrids and species, both large- and small-flowered, including viticellas and Jackmanii-type hybrids. These clematis can be pruned very hard, if necessary. They are likely to have a rather ugly profusion of old flowering stems at the end of the summer and these can be removed to tidy the plant, leaving the harsher pruning until later in the winter, or when the first signs of new growth appear. Left unpruned, they will all still flower but these blooms are likely to appear among the previous year's unsightly tangle of old and frequently dead flowering stems. In most cases, it is best to prune the plant back to within 30cm of the ground at this time.

Within this group, the texensis, integrifolia and herbaceous clematis will naturally die down to the main crown, while the heracleifolias die down to a knobbly woody rootstock. Others in this group, like the viticellas, the Jackmanii types and the orientalis group, can form perennial woody stems and do not die down to the ground, except in extremely cold winters.

After the autumn tidy-up, you should wait for the first signs of new growth in late winter to early spring, before pruning. The advantage of waiting is that in some cases you may not want to cut these clematis all the way down to within 30cm of the ground, as is often recommended, but prune them a little higher up the plant instead. This is particularly convenient where these types have been trained against a wall or grown through a planting of mixed shrubs and perennials, where old stems already weave among their host plants. Simply cut to above the strongest and most strategically placed shoots.

Clematis in the orientalis group do not need to be cut all the way down to the ground either. You can get away with giving them a quick trim with hedging shears, shearing the old flowering shoots back to their main stems and back to the emerging new buds.

MIDSUMMER PRUNING AND DEADHEADING

Unless you are particularly fond of the seedheads of large-flowered hybrids, it would be worth removing spent flowers in midsummer, and even cutting back some of the old shoots. This will stimulate some new shoots that may carry more flowers later in the season. This practice should be accompanied by generous feeding and watering (see pages 144–45). If you grow clematis alongside roses, the deadheading and feeding can be practised on both at the same time, straight after the first flourish of flowers.

I have also hard-pruned mildew-prone clematis like 'Romantika' and some of the texensis types in midsummer when they have been badly infected by the disease. The subsequent new growth is often disease-free and strong enough to flower again by early autumn.

training

Unlike sweet peas, which have tendrils, wisteria, which twines, or even ivy, with self-clinging roots attached to the stem, clematis twist their leaf petioles around anything they can find. Especially adapted to grip the twiggy branches of shrubs, this form of attachment has not evolved to cope with larger branches or thick poles, but will eagerly grapple with wire and fine mesh of all kinds. If you have provided your clematis with a grid to cling to, then no training may be necessary. It can be left to romp away until it reaches the top of the frame or support plant.

STARTING THEM OFF

A newly planted clematis may need help on the first part of its journey from the cane provided by the nursery to whatever its support structure is going to be. It is best to untie the plant from its original cane, spacing out the shoots which are often bunched too tightly together. Fan out this growth by tying it on to two or three longer canes. If you have to plant the clematis some distance from a tree, use a long cane or a secure guy wire to help it into the tree's lower branches.

A few vertical wires running up the posts will be enough to get a clematis to climb up an arbour or pergola. Netting can also be wrapped around the posts, provided it is not too unsightly. On obelisks, gather all the shoots together and wrap them in a tight spiral around the structure to foster a more floriferous plant.

A well-trained plant like 'Warszawska Nike' will repeat-flower from mid- to late summer, obscuring the obelisk with its blooms.

TRAINING ON AN OBELISK

1 *A combination of canes and ropes makes an ideal support. This attractive obelisk is made of oak laths tied together with sisal rope.*

2 *Clematis tend to flower near the top of a support so, to obtain a full-looking plant, train the growth in spirals around the obelisk.*

3 *Initially tie the growths on with string or wire, using small wire ties. These will rust and fall away as the plant starts to support itself.*

1 Without support, clematis shoots cling to each other, forming bundles that often hang down in swathes.

2 Here a swathe has been lifted up onto a single wire strained between vine eyes in the wall. Initially the clematis will need tying on to the wire but it will soon find its own way, given a supportive framework.

3 The twining leaf petioles wind once or twice around twigs, wires or canes (but not around poles or canes thicker than 2cm).

AGAINST A WALL

To prepare a wall to receive a clematis you will need to attach to it several wires, some netting or trellis. A mesh of 10–15cm squares is ideal. Fine chicken wire is not advisable as it will become impossible to separate the clematis from it when it comes to pruning. To wire a wall for clematis and roses, fix the wires in a grid 60cm square, using strong vine eyes. If you tie the main shoots on to the face of the wire, it will be easier to take them off at a later date. Clematis shoots tend to cling together, so provided that there is a good framework underneath, the clematis will fill the gaps with stray and hanging shoots, which will bind together.

Some large-flowered hybrids, like 'Marie Boisselot' and 'W. E Gladstone' tend to flower only at the top of their very tall growth. To encourage them to flower lower down, simply train some shoots back down or farther out sideways.

Lanky herbaceous clematis like *C. × diversifolia*, which do not have twining petioles, will need to be tucked behind wires or into other plants in order to stay up, otherwise they will need regular tying in. Do not worry about snapping some shoots when attaching or training clematis, as they regenerate rapidly and readily.

IN BORDERS

You need to do little or nothing to help a clematis grow into a shrub and through a border, except to guide them in the early stages of growth. Unless you want them to grow on a particular side of a specific plant, it would be best just to let them do as they will. Separating out the shoots will, however, prevent some plants from forming heavy mats of growth on top of small shrubs.

Old viticella plants can be a problem when they are hard pruned to within 30cm of the ground, because this stimulates them to generate a tower of 20–30 new shoots each year. If these are not tackled, they may fall in a self-embracing pile in the wrong direction, possibly collapsing on a precious plant in the process. If left until too late in the summer, it may be tricky to pull the shoots apart. As you really need only six to eight good shoots to spread out through a border or into a shrub, it is best to separate the shoots in spring, when they are 60–100cm high. Although several will break in the process, you will still be left with more than enough shoots to train.

If you wish to keep these shoots on the ground to weave among low-growing plants, peg them down for their first 2–3m with small, hand-made wire hooks (a 15cm length of wire, bent at one end) to prevent them from lurching up into unsuspecting shrubs. Trained this way, some viticella shoots may reach 5m. If this is too long, simply pinch out the tips of these shoots. You may also peg down some shoots of large-flowered hybrids, montanas and other woody-stemmed clematis, and these may, in a year or two, naturally produce roots and subsequently a new plant (see Layering, pages 149–50).

feeding and watering

In the wild, clematis behave like free-range opportunists, happy to haunt the base of other plants. In ecological terms, this earns them a place among the tough 'pioneer' vegetation. It would be wrong, however, to assume that they have an unlimited ability to fend for themselves and to survive on scraps. Treated in this way, they will soon, like ill-prepared hikers in the wilderness, look malnourished and frail and may wither away altogether.

FEEDING

Clematis need food right from the start, so good preparation at the time of planting is the key. I recently planted out a measly pot-bound *C. montana* whose roots had been partially eaten by vine weevil grubs. Removing all the soil from around the plant's roots, I tucked the clematis in a mixture of one part well-rotted manure to three parts soil, hoping for little more than a few new shoots. By the end of the summer this frail creature had grown to cover 4m² of wall! *C. montana* is a naturally vigorous species but this generous encouragement had paid high dividends. The same year, a similar but healthier plant hastily thrown into some unenriched, rather parched soil near a tree, grew only one-tenth of the size.

Well-rotted manure should always be thoroughly mixed in with soil removed from the planting hole. Never simply throw a lump or two into the bottom of the hole, hoping that the plant will happily devour it, nor imagine that these few lumps will sustain the plant forever. The key to sustained nourishment is a good, thick layer of manure on top of the soil every year. Placed around the base of the plant in early autumn, this will act not only as a slow-release fertilizer but also as a moisture-retentive mulch for the rest of the year.

When I took over a clematis collection ten years ago, I asked gardener and writer Christopher Lloyd for advice. All he had to say to me was 'Feed them!' He was right. Tired old specimens perk up beautifully with a dose of manure. Treat clematis as you would a rose: plant it well and feed it generously every year.

Feeding during the growing season is also to be recommended, especially after a midsummer deadheading or pruning. For a quick energy fix, use a tomato-formula liquid feed or liquid seaweed. Beware of applying it too late in the summer, as this will stimulate soft growth that will not have time to harden up enough to withstand the rigours of winter.

For container plants and to give garden plants a boost, water with a diluted liquid feed of a seaweed-based fertilizer, or use a fertilizer formulated for tomatoes.

FEEDING CONTAINER PLANTS

These same liquid feeds are also ideal for container plants, which should be dosed once a month beginning just before the start of the growing season and continuing until midsummer. Another way to invigorate a container plant is to scrape out, using your fingers, the top 6–10cm of the existing potting compost in late winter, trying not to damage the roots. Then topdress the container with fresh compost. In Japan, where large-flowered clematis are frequently grown in relatively small 3–5 litre pots, gardeners sometimes remove all the soil after a plant has flowered in early summer, then cut the plant back and re-pot it. After such a drastic treatment, needless to say the clematis will need a good soaking.

WATERING

For the majority of clematis, water is crucial, especially in their first few years. In a dry season, it is a good idea to give clematis 5–10 litres a week while they get established. Here again, clematis show a remarkable similarity to roses which also need plenty of food and water, especially in the early part of the growing season, to give of their best. Once you have planted your clematis and given it a thorough soaking, you should consider its aftercare. If it is inconvenient to drag a hose or watering can over to your new plant, then the use of a mulch will prove valuable, but not a substitute.

In the garden a thick layer of well-rotted manure, applied in spring or autumn, will act as a slow-release fertilizer and moisture-retentive mulch.

COVERING THE ROOTS

There are many theories about what to lay over the roots of clematis. The important thing to remember is that the roots should always be kept moist, bearing in mind that in the wild plants such as *C. montana* and *C. koreana* are moist woodland dwellers. It has been said that the roots should remain in cool shade – cool, yes, but moisture is much more important. It would be better to have the roots in full sun and kept moist than to be in the dry shade of a wall.

To keep the roots cool, many gardeners place stones on the soil around them. This does help but it is also the perfect abode for slugs, snails, earwigs and even mice, all happy to venture out from their shelter to climb up the clematis for a midnight snack. A light-coloured sharp grit or gravel is preferable to stones, but liquid feeding would then be necessary, as manure and grit do not mix well.

Certain clematis, on the other hand, like it hot and dry. The orientalis group are surprisingly drought-tolerant. *C. flammula* and its offspring, *C. × aromatica* and *C. × triternata* 'Rubromarginata', prefer a well-drained, sunny position. Given too much water, they will grow very lush and may collapse. Other dry-loving clematis include *C. cirrhosa*, *C. recta*, the orientalis group and all the New Zealanders. The latter, like many evergreens, prefer it on the dry side in winter but do enjoy moisture during the growing season.

pests and diseases

The majority of clematis species and the small-flowered hybrids are quite trouble-free and are rarely visited by pests or diseases. But the large-flowered hybrids, perhaps through excessive breeding, are more liable to be plagued by the attentions of pests, and are particularly susceptible to the one major disease of clematis, clematis wilt. Treatments for most of these are readily available and none of them is too drastic.

CLEMATIS WILT

Wilt generally afflicts only the large-flowered hybrids, though it has caused heartache to many a gardener. The symptoms of this fungal disease can occur at any time, from spring to late summer. An infected plant appears to be in perfect health, flush with flowers and plump, opening buds, only to collapse suddenly, showing symptoms akin to those of drought. The entire plant droops, before turning blackish brown in a few days.

The disease usually enters stems through infected leaves in a cool, wet season. Plants with tough, undamaged bark will stand a better chance than those which have already been damaged by slugs, mice or accident. The most susceptible varieties are to be found among the early-flowering hybrids, like 'Vyvyan Pennel', 'Duchess of Edinburgh' and 'Marie Boisselot', while others, like 'Hagley Hybrid' and 'Ville de Lyon', are among the more resistant. Most viticellas are fairly immune, too, so if any of these collapse, do not be hasty in blaming wilt.

No fungicide is labelled for use against wilt in the U.K. today. The only remedy is a radical one – all the infected growth should be pruned close to ground level, then removed and burned. The disease attacks the plant at any point down to ground level but rarely below it. This is why it is recommended that wilt-prone clematis should be planted at least 7.5cm deep. Usually the buds that remain buried will be able to regenerate, whereas a plant that has not been planted deep enough may be killed outright. Do not give up on a plant that has been killed down to ground level but does not sprout again in the next season. They have been known to reappear suddenly the following year, or even after a few years.

Clematis showing the same symptoms as wilt may have been affected by other causes. A wilted-looking plant may simply have been broken or cut, nipped off by a mouse or rabbit or, most commonly, had its bark stripped by slugs or snails.

PHYTOPHTHORA

Whereas wilt affects the upper stems of clematis, *Phytophthora* is a fungus that tends to devastate the roots systems of plants, causing the leaves to turn brown as if stressed from lack of water. This is a rare disease which occurs most often in hot, wet summers. *C. heracleifolia* and the atragenes, particularly those grown in pots, are most commonly affected. There are fungicidal treatments for amateur gardeners.

SLIME FLUX

This rare bacterial disease mostly affects *C. montana*. A foul-smelling creamy froth oozes from cracked stems, usually in spring after the last frosts. As with wilt, cut down the affected growth and destroy it. Plants usually recover, with new shoots bursting from below the damage.

MILDEW

Mildew, a disfiguring fungal disease which develops during dry, mild weather, affects many plants including clematis. Members of the texensis group are especially prone to mildew, as well as a few late-flowering Jackmanii types like 'Romantika' and 'Viola'. The most visible symptom is a grey-white powdery substance developing on the stems; this soon spreads to the leaves and, in severe cases, spoils the flowers too.

Powdery and downy mildews can infect the leaves and flowers of many clematis, especially in dry summers with cool nights.

The only really effective way to control mildew is through the use of preventative fungicides, as spraying fungicide after the infection has taken hold produces only limited results. If the outbreak is really severe, it is best to cut the whole plant down to the ground, where it should sprout again. Given a long, late summer these new shoots may even flower again, usually completely mildew-free. Reducing water stress by watering and mulching is another useful preventative measure.

PESTS

Slugs and snails can be destructive pests, stripping the bark off

Snails eat the bark of clematis, often causing a plant to collapse. Together with slugs, they are the worst enemy of clematis.

old stems and eating succulent new shoots. Slugs nibble the shoots near to ground level, but snails can climb into the upper reaches of a plant. Control slugs and snails by hand removal at night, or scatter slug pellets around the plant. Biological control with a pathogenic nematode is available for slugs.

MICE AND RABBITS

Mice will also climb clematis and eat both flower buds and tender shoots. Clematis grown against old brick and stone walls are vulnerable because walls, like old tree stumps and rocks, can provide ideal hiding places for mice and snails. Hard-pruned clematis can be persistently chewed off by mice and rabbits, and never get a chance to grow strongly. Cats, traps and poisonous bait are some of the remedies. Covering the stems of clematis with wire netting will prevent rabbits from damaging the stems of clematis.

EARWIGS

Earwigs hide in the daytime but clamber up clematis shoots at night, where they delight in chewing leaves, shoots and flowers to shreds. They can be caught by leaving balls of straw or hay in

Earwigs emerge at night, chomping and shredding leaves and flowers. The symptoms can be confused with slug damage.

pots near the plant and collecting them during the day. Visiting your clematis at night with a torch, you may find slugs, snails and earwigs all enjoying a hearty midnight snack. Pluck them off and drop them in salted water to destroy them.

VINE WEEVILS

Vine weevils are a recent problem for gardeners – a by-product of intensive nursery production. Although the adult beetles do some damage at night by notching out pieces from leaves, the real menace comes from the white maggot-like larvae, which voraciously devour plant roots. The roots of container-grown young plants grown in light composts are especially easy for them to negotiate, and they will often consume the entire root system, killing the plant. Bare-rooted plants grown in heavier soils are less susceptible. As a precaution, drench container-grown plants with one of the new systemic insecticide products or use biological control with a pathogenic nematode.

OTHER TROUBLES

Clematis may be visited by aphids, red spider mites and leaf miners but major debilitating infestations are rare. Birds and

Leaf miners disfigure the leaves of clematis but rarely do enough damage to warrant treatment.

caterpillars may eat the swelling buds of early-flowering clematis. On some large-flowered clematis, the first flowers to open may be green. This is usually due to their buds having been exposed to prolonged cold in spring. Later flowers will tend to revert to their normal colouring. Browning leaves on *C. armandii* are usually caused by cold winds – remove them if they are unsightly.

propagation

Until the 1950s, the usual method of propagating clematis was by grafting shoots on to the rootstocks of *C. vitalba* or *C. viticella*. This relatively laborious method is rarely practised today in commerce, as most clematis can be successfully raised from cuttings. New varieties and rare species may initially have been raised from seed, but once a grower has established a plant with unique features that he or she wishes to preserve, seed collected from it will not produce identical offspring. To raise plants that are genetically identical to the new plant he or she will have to propagate them asexually, from cuttings, divisions or layering.

While some clematis species germinate rapidly in their first year, others may take a year or more. If the seedlings are small and not too crowded, they may be left in the pot until the second spring before pricking them out and potting them on.

GROWING FROM SEED

Clematis set seed quite readily in gardens and are fairly easy to propagate in this way. Amateurs and professionals the world over are trying this out in their greenhouses and cold frames. Since the large-flowered clematis, in particular, are of such mixed blood, the result from seed sowing is infinitely variable. Of the new varieties offered for sale each year, most differ only slightly from the clematis already available. Many an enthusiast wants to believe that he or she has raised something special, perhaps longing to name a plant after themselves, a relative or a friend. These new introductions are now scrutinized by nurserymen and by

SOWING SEEDS

1 *Spread the seed evenly over the surface of a pot filled with loam-based seed-sowing compost. The feathery styles can be trimmed off carefully, but this is not necessary.*

2 *Cover the seeds with a thin layer of vermiculite or sharp grit to help retain moisture and to reflect heat. This covering will also discourage moss and liverworts, which can choke young seedlings.*

3 *Label the pot of seeds and place in a cool position, out of direct sun, in the garden or an unheated greenhouse or cold frame. Ensure that the germinating seeds stay moist and guard against attacks by slugs and mice.*

1 *In autumn or late winter, prune down the clump of a herbaceous plant such as this* C. tubulosa *'Wyevale'. Dig up the whole clump, or just part of it, using a fork or a sharp spade.*

2 *Using a spade, chop the clump into generous pieces that can either be re-planted the size they are or divided even further.*

3 *To divide further, tease out pieces with your hands. A small clump can yield dozens of small rooted pieces that can each be potted up or replanted in a nursery bed.*

specialist societies, the majority fading into obscurity. Each year may throw up only one or two that offer a genuine breakthrough and have real staying power.

For the amateur, however, growing a clematis from seed can be an exciting adventure. The seed collected from garden hybrids will yield progeny of a complex and varied genetic mix. One or two may show some unique colouring or a shape worthy of being introduced as a new named variety, but most will be kept merely as a token of the grower's personal triumph or eventually discarded.

Collect the seeds as they ripen in autumn, when the individual fruits at the base of their individual feathery styles turn brown and separate easily from the main seedhead. Clematis seed are best sown fresh in a cold greenhouse or cold frame during autumn but may be stored and sown early in the following spring. A few seedlings may appear in the first spring but some may take two years to germinate. Young plants should be handled with great care for their first year.

Wild-collected seed of the species, especially of the orientalis group, will tend to produce plants that are true to type, whereas seedlings collected from garden plants of an improved form, like 'Lambton Park', should not be passed off as true 'Lambton Park'. The orientalis group are so easy to raise from seed that some growers prefer to propagate them this way, leaking unimpressive forms of species like *C. flammula* and *C. tangutica* into commerce. All the best forms of these species should be raised by asexual means, in other words from cuttings, layers or divisions.

DIVISION

Division is the simplest way to increase stock of herbaceous clematis like *C. recta*, *C. heracleifolia* and *C. integrifolia*. In autumn or late winter, hearty clumps can be lifted and broken into several pieces. The larger divisions may be replanted right away but any small side-shoots with an inkling of root on them can be potted up and nurtured until they are large enough to be planted out.

Many clematis, including the orientalis group and the atragenes, generate a number of suckers, especially if they have been planted deep. Rather than lifting the entire plant, it may be possible to find a shoot or two with a few rootlets attached. Remove each one with a sharp knife and pot it up. Even some of the large-flowered clematis can be propagated in this way.

LAYERING

Layering is the easiest and least time-consuming way to produce one or two plants of most clematis, except the herbaceous kind, whose stems tend to die back. A clematis that develops woody stems may be layered at any time of year, but late winter is best. Some plants may even generate natural layers of their own.

Scoop out a small hole in the ground, then bury a 15cm length of woody stem 4–8cm deep into the hole – or into a pot buried with its rim at ground level. Secure the stem in the ground with a piece of wire or a stone and cover with moistened compost. Finally, insert a cane and label it, otherwise you may forget where it is and what you have done. Within 12-18 months you may cut the umbilical cord – the main stem that connects the stem to the parent plant – and dig up your new plant. If only a few roots have been produced, simply pot it up and leave until the roots have filled a 2-litre container.

GROWING FROM CUTTINGS

In spring, commercial growers take semi-ripe cuttings – neither too soft nor too hard – from very young plants that have been grown under cover. These cuttings are then placed in a suitable cutting medium, like perlite, in trays over bottom heat (18-20°C). They are then covered with a clear light plastic sheet and shaded. The amateur grower should imitate these nursery techniques as closely as possible. Cuttings can be taken from garden plants in late spring to early summer, as soon as the growth is firm enough. Insert them in a pot or a seed tray in a propagator. It will be harder to establish cuttings taken later in the summer; they will root but the young plantlets may simply fade away during the long winter.

A cutting taken in its prime will, with the aid of a hormone rooting medium, root in six to eight weeks. The cutting may be wounded by slicing off a sliver of bark from the base, to increase the surface area that will produce roots. If the cutting has rooted by midsummer, you can pot it up immediately into a 9cm pot in some light compost. It will then have a month or two to become established as a young plant, able to withstand the rigours of winter. If rooting takes place later in the summer, do not disturb the cuttings but leave them in their tray or pot in a greenhouse and feed them once with a light liquid feed, before potting them on the following spring. It is important to observe stringent hygiene at every stage, by applying fungicides and removing any dead leaves or rotting cuttings.

Young potted cuttings should be nurtured, not over-watered, and potted on into a 2-litre container as soon as the new roots have filled the 9cm pot. If you can keep the young plant in a greenhouse, you will have a fine plant ready to take on the outside world in 18–24 months.

TYPES OF CUTTING

The most popular type is the internodal cutting, partly out of economy of material, and because the distance between some nodes is so long as to make the cutting ungainly (varieties like 'Perle d'Azur' have internodes up to 50cm long). In some countries nodal cuttings are the preferred type, cutting once above the upper node and just below the lower one. This method doubles the chances of securing a young rooted plant should the top set of buds die from cold and

Raise a single plant by simply pinning a shoot down into a pot plunged into the soil. Mulch and keep it moist at all times, then after a year or so, cut the old shoot and lift the pot.

This rootball of an atragene shows how natural suckers can be produced, even on a young plant. These can be carefully prised off and potted up separately.

In autumn, hardwood cuttings of some clematis can be made from nodal cuttings, like this one.

works well for herbaceous types like *C. heracleifolia* and hollow-stemmed species like *C. recta*. Montanas and atragenes are the easiest groups to root from semi-ripe cuttings while large-flowered hybrids tend to have a lower success rate.

The amateur who needs to grow only one or two new plants may prefer to take hardwood cuttings in early autumn, a method that requires far less intensive care. *C. montana* and *C. heracleifolia* types will root well enough this way, using internodal or nodal cuttings about 10cm long. Wound them and dip in rooting hormone gel before inserting them in a cutting mix in a pot or tray. Keep them in an unheated greenhouse, shaded from excess sun. Continue to water in winter.

TAKING SEMI-RIPE CUTTINGS

1 *Select a healthy long shoot in late spring or early summer. The best material is neither too soft nor too hard. This shoot should yield four or five cuttings.*

2 *For an internodal cutting, make the first clean cut 2–4cm below a node, using a very sharp knife or razor blade. Secateurs can often damage a cutting by crushing the bark.*

3 *Make the second cut immediately above the node, then cut some of the leaf back. If there are two leaves, remove one of them.*

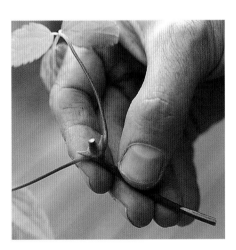

4 *For cuttings taken from harder wood, 'wound' the cutting by slicing off a sliver of bark near the base, then dip the tip of the cutting into some rooting hormone gel.*

5 *Push the cuttings into a potful of 'cuttings' compost, burying the node slightly. The compost can be a specially formulated mix or plain perlite.*

6 *Place the pot of cuttings into a propagator or cover it with a plastic bag. Place the pot over some bottom heat (up to 20°C). Keep it moist, shaded and hygienic.*

hybridization

Gardeners continue in the relentless pursuit of new forms and colours in flowers, as if nature herself had not provided enough already. This they do through a mix of art and chance, in the hope of a new perfection derived from the hybridizing of two species or varieties. It is surprising how many so-called new hybrids were from uncontrolled sources and not from deliberately chosen parents. Although such a random approach might produce a rare surprise, careful choice of parents will increase your chances of something special.

In the wild, species are naturally variable, as variability is a tool for survival. Plants grown from seed collected in the wild may be special and can be given a name, and this selection should be propagated by asexual means only – that is, by cuttings or layers, but not from seed.

There are three levels to the craft of raising a new cultivar. The first is the most random, by simply collecting seed from a garden plant that has been exposed to many sources of pollen, and hoping for the best. The second is to isolate the mother plant from all except one of her prospective suitors. A good place to do this would be a closed greenhouse, where the vents have been covered over with gauze to prevent bees from bringing in pollen from outside. The last and most labour-intensive way is to de-masculate the mother plant by removing the stamens, and bringing to her, under strictly controlled conditions, pollen from a carefully chosen, compatible male plant. The products of these endeavours should be judiciously selected, then propagated by asexual means. The resulting new hybrid cultivars should continue to be propagated by asexual means only so that each new plant grown from it will be a clone with identical genetic make-up.

CREATING A NEW CLEMATIS

1 *Select a flower on the mother plant and, using sharp scissors, cut off the sepals just as they are about to open.*

2 *Carefully trim off the 'male' stamens that surround the 'female' stigma.*

3 *Using a soft-bristled paintbrush, collect some fresh pollen from the 'father' plant.*

4 *Transfer the pollen to the ripening style, which should be slightly sticky, and repeat the process over the course of a few days.*

5 *Cover the stigma with a muslin 'hood' for a week or two to prevent fertilization by foreign pollen. Wait for the seeds to ripen.*

Herbaceous clematis like 'Edward Prichard' naturally produce long, straight stems that are ideal for cut flowers, but virtually any clematis could be used in this way.

Picked fresh and treated correctly, clematis flowers may last a week or more in water. Look for flowers that have just opened or are three-quarters open, at the point when the sepals are about to reach their full size, but before the stamens start to unfold.

Sports differ from hybrids, deriving as they do from odd shoots that deviate from the parent plant by 'sporting' a new colour or shape of flower or leaf. Since a sport has a tendency to revert back to its parent plant, new plants raised from cuttings or layers of these deviant shoots should be grown for some years to prove that they are inherently stable. 'Multi Blue', for example, is relatively stable but still capable of producing flowers identical to those of its parent, 'The President'.

A new trend in the last two decades has been the patenting of new varieties, which bars anyone from propagating them except under licence from the patent holder. Although not in the usual spirit of generosity shown by gardeners, who have always freely exchanged plants, even the amateur must abide by these rules.

cut flowers

Ernest Markham, William Robinson's head gardener, wrote in his book *Clematis* as long ago as 1935 that he 'heartily recommends' these flowers of 'unusual charm and distinction' for cutting. In Japan and the USA there has recently been a minor revival of clematis as a commercial cut flower. Some pioneers at Chalk Hill nursery near San Francisco in California have been experimenting with over 80 varieties, which is a good indication of the possibilities.

Those lovely but lanky herbaceous types, like 'Alionushka' and *C.* × *durandii*, while slightly awkward in the garden, come into their own as cut flowers as they carry their blooms on long, straight stems and will flower again after being cut. *C. heracleifolia* and its forms all make excellent cut flowers too, as their growth is similar in habit to more conventional cut flowers, with stiff and erect stems producing whorls of outward-facing tubular flowers, with the added bonus of exquisite fragrance. But why not take advantage of the unique habit of clematis, by allowing trails of *C. montana* or *C. alpina* to hang down from shelves or windowsills? Clematis seedheads too are wonderful as part of a late-summer or autumnal flower arrangement, but they must be picked before the fluffy stage.

Clematis grown especially for cut flowers are best pruned hard to encourage long stems and need to be well-fed. Whereas commerce demands a shelf life of at least seven to ten days, we may pick an open flower and stick it into a vase, or float it in a bowl, in the hope that it might last three to four days. But if cut at the optimum time, clematis flowers could last up to 14 days in water.

To prepare clematis well for cutting, take the bucket to the garden and choose thick, strong stems with a woody base, as soft stems will soon collapse. For optimum freshness, dip stem tips in a little boiling water for a few seconds. Remove some foliage to reduce transpiration, immerse as much of the stem as you can in cold water, then leave in a cool, dark place overnight. The next day the stems can be re-cut to the desired length.

CLEMATIS BY COLOUR

WHITE

PLANT NAME	FLR SIZE	SEASON
EVERGREENS	Small	Spring
C. armandii	Small	Spring
C. paniculata	Small	Spring
'Avalanche'	Small	Spring
ATRAGENES		
'White Columbine'	Small	Spring
'White Moth'	Small	Spring
MONTANAS		
var. grandiflora	Small	Spring
var. wilsonii	Small	Spring
C. spooneri	Small	Spring
LARGE-FLOWERED HYBRIDS		
Arctic Queen	Large	Early summer
'Miss Bateman'	Large	Early summer
'Gillian Blades'	Large	Early summer
'Marie Boisselot'	Large	Early summer
'Henryi'	Large	Early summer
'Snow Queen'	Large	Early summer
LATE SPECIES/HYBRIDS		
'Alba Luxurians'	Small	Mid-late summer
C. integrifolia 'Alba'	Small	Mid-late summer
C. potaninii	Small	Mid-late summer
C. flammula	Small	Mid-late summer
'Paul Farges'	Small	Mid-late summer
'Anita'	Small	Mid-late summer
C. recta	Small	Mid-late summer
'Kaiu'	Small	Mid-late summer
C. terniflora	Small	Mid-late summer
C. vitalba	Small	Mid-late summer
'Huldine'	Large	Mid-late summer
'John Huxtable'	Large	Mid-late summer

GREEN TO CREAM

EVERGREENS		
C. cirrhosa 'Ourika Valley'	Small	Winter
C. cirrhosa 'Wisley Cream'	Small	Winter
'Jingle Bells'	Small	Winter
C. marmoraria	Small	Spring
'Pixie'	Small	Spring
C. forsteri	Small	Spring
'Primrose Star'	Small	Spring
LARGE-FLOWERED HYBRIDS		
Wada's Primrose	Large	Early summer
'Moonlight'	Large	Early summer
'Guernsey Cream'	Large	Early summer
'Duchess of Edinburgh'	Large	Early summer
LATE SPECIES/ HYBRIDS		
C. rehderiana	Small	Mid-late summer
'Hagelby White'	Small	Mid-late summer

LEMON- TO ORANGE-YELLOW

C. chiisanensis 'Lovechild'	Small	Spring
'Shiva'	Small	Spring
LATE SPECIES/ HYBRIDS		
'Bill MacKenzie'	Small	Mid-late summer
'Lambton Park'	Small	Mid-late summer
'Helios'	Small	Mid-late summer
Golden Tiara	Small	Mid-late summer
'My Angel'	Small	Mid-late summer
C. ladakhiana	Small	Mid-late summer

RED TO DEEP PURPLE-RED

'Ernest Markham'	Large	Early summer
'Sunset'	Large	Early summer
'Niobe'	Large	Early summer
'Westerplatte'	Large	Early summer
LATE SPECIES/HYBRIDS		
'Kermesina'	Small	Mid-late summer
C. texensis	Small	Mid-late summer
'Gravetye Beauty'	Small	Mid-late summer
'Madame Edouard André'	Large	Mid-late summer
'Rouge Cardinal'	Large	Mid-late summer

PINK

EVERGREEN		
C. armandii 'Apple Blossom'	Small	Spring
ATRAGENES		
'Markham's Pink'	Small	Spring
'Constance'	Small	Spring
'Ballet Skirt'	Small	Spring
'Rosy O'Grady'	Small	Spring
'Willy'	Small	Spring
'Columella'	Small	Spring
MONTANAS		
'Elizabeth'	Small	Spring
C. chrysochoma	Small	Spring
'Pink Perfection'	Small	Spring
LARGE-FLOWERED HYBRIDS		
Josephine	Large	Early summer
'Mrs Spencer Castle'	Large	Early summer
LATE SPECIES/HYBRIDS		
'Pastel Pink'	Small	Mid-late summer
'Heather Herschell'	Small	Mid-late summer
'Duchess of Albany'	Small	Mid-late summer
'Comtesse de Bouchaud'	Large	Mid-late summer

DEEP PINK TO PURPLE-PINK

MONTANAS		
'Tetrarose'	Small	Spring
'Freda'	Small	Spring
var. rubens	Small	Spring
'Broughton Star'	Small	Spring
LARGE-FLOWERED HYBRIDS		
'Jackmanii Rubra'	Large	Early summer
Pink Champagne	Large	Early summer
'Asao'	Large	Early summer
LATE SPECIES/ HYBRIDS		
'Abundance'	Small	Mid-late summer
'Princess Diana'	Small	Mid-late summer
'Madame Julia Correvon'	Small	Mid-late summer
'Étoile Rose'	Small	Mid-late summer
'Alionushka'	Small	Mid-late summer
'Minuet'	Small	Mid-late summer
'Ville de Lyon'	Large	Mid-late summer
'Hagley Hybrid'	Large	Mid-late summer
'Margaret Hunt'	Large	Mid-late summer

PURPLE TO VIOLET-PURPLE

ATRAGENES		
'Brunette'	Small	Spring
'Helsingborg'	Small	Spring
'Tage Lundell'	Small	Spring
LARGE-FLOWERED HYBRIDS		
'The President'	Large	Early summer
'Multi Blue'	Large	Early summer

PURPLE TO VIOLET-PURPLE (CONT'D)

'Burma Star'	Large	Early summer
'The Vagabond'	Large	Early summer
LATE SPECIES/HYBRIDS		
'Black Prince'	Small	Mid-late summer
'Étoile Violette'	Small	Mid-late summer
C. viticella 'Flore Pleno'	Small	Mid-ate summer
'Royal Velours'	Small	Mid-late summer
'Purpurea Plena Elegans'	Small	Mid-late summer
'Venosa Violacea'	Small	Mid-late summer
'Jackmanii'	Large	Mid-late summer
'Jackmanii Superba'	Large	Mid-late summer
'Gipsy Queen'	Large	Mid-late summer
'Romantika'	Large	Mid-late summer

MID- TO DARK BLUE

ATRAGENES		
'Frances Rivis'	Small	Spring
C. macropetala	Large	Spring
'Pamela Jackman'	Small	Spring
LARGE-FLOWERED HYBRIDS		
'Beauty of Worcester'	Large	Early summer
'Countess of Lovelace'	Large	Early summer
'Daniel Deronda'	Large	Early summer
'Elsa Späth'	Large	Early summer
'Lady Northcliffe'	Large	Early summer
'Lasurstern'	Large	Early summer
'Mrs Cholmondeley'	Large	Early summer
'Ramona'	Large	Early summer
'Vyvyan Pennell'	Large	Early summer
'William Kennett'	Large	Early summer
'Arabella'	Small	Mid-late summer
Blue Rain	Small	Mid-late summer
C. x durandii	Small	Mid-late summer
C. x eriostemon	Small	Mid-late summer
C. integrifolia	Small	Mid-late summer
Harlow Carr	Small	Mid-late summer
C. tubulosa 'Wyevale'	Small	Mid-late summer
'Perle d'Azur'	Large	Mid-late summer
'Prince Charles'	Large	Mid-late summer
'Rhapsody'	Large	Mid-late summer
Wisley	Large	Mid-late summer
'Victoria'	Large	Mid-late summer

LIGHT BLUE AND PALE MAUVE-BLUE

ATRAGENES		
'Blue Bird'	Small	Spring
LARGE-FLOWERED HYBRIDS		
C. patens	Large	Early summer
'Louise Rowe'	Large	Early summer
'Chalcedony'	Large	Early summer
'Belle of Woking'	Large	Early summer
'Fujimusume'	Large	Early summer
'H. F. Young'	Large	Early summer
'Will Goodwin'	Large	Early summer
'General Sikorski'	Large	Early summer
LATE SPECIES/HYBRIDS		
'Betty Corning'	Small	Mid-late summer
C. integrifolia	Small	Mid-late summer
'Pastel Blue'	Small	Mid-late summer
'Pagoda'	Small	Mid-late summer
'Praecox'	Small	Mid-late summer
'Mrs Robert Brydon'	Small	Mid-late summer
Blue Angel	Large	Mid-late summer

SPECIAL USES AND SITUATIONS

fragrant clematis

The following clematis have a fragrance that carries, especially under warm, sunny conditions. Some, like 'Betty Corning' and a few atragenes,have a faint scent but only when inhaled closely, and some claim can be made by large-flowered hybrids like 'Fair Rosamund' and 'Rhapsody' but this, I believe, is a bit far-fetched. Certainly none of these is worth including for its scent alone, but the following certainly are.

WINTER
C. cirrhosa, especially indoors

SPRING
C. forsteri,'Pixie' and 'Lunar Lass' (New Zealanders)
C. armandii and all forms, including 'Apple Blossom and 'Little White Charm'
C. montana and 'Elizabeth', C. montana var. rubens 'Odorata', 'Elten', 'Tetrarose', 'Mayleen', 'Fragrant Spring'

SUMMER
C. tubulosa ' Wyevale', 'New Love';
C. flammula and derivatives;
C. x aromatica, C. triternata 'Rubromarginata', C. rehderiana

additional pruning notes

The following clematis in Pruning Group Two will reliably flower later if pruned hard (that is, if treated as Group Three), rather than the usual way of light pruning:

'Niobe', 'Warszawska Nike', 'The President', 'The Bride', 'Pink Fantasy', 'Multi Blue', 'Fujimusume', 'William Kennett'

clematis for special conditions

FOR COLD AND SHADE
All alpinas and all macropetalas
Most montanas (but not C. chrysochoma and derivatives)
'Carnaby', 'Comtesse de Bouchaud', 'Dawn', 'Fireworks',' Fujimusume', 'Hagley Hybrid', 'Henryi', 'Lincoln Star', 'Margaret Hunt', 'Moonlight', 'Nelly Moser', 'Prince Charles', 'Sunset', 'Victoria', 'William Kennett', Wada's Primrose

clematis for containers and small gardens

SPRING
All atragenes
All New Zealanders

SUMMER
Arctic Queen, C. x aromatica, 'Burma Star', 'Carnaby', 'Elsa Späth', C. florida and derivatives, 'Fujimusume', 'Gillian Blades', Josephine, 'Lady Northcliffe',' Lasurstern', 'Madame Julia Correvon', 'Multi Blue', 'Niobe', Petit Faucon, Pink Champagne, 'Pink Fantasy', 'Prince Charles', 'Princess Diana', 'Ramona', 'Rhapsody', 'Snow Queen','First Lady', 'The President', 'Venosa Violacea', 'Ville de Lyon', 'Warszawska Nike', 'Westerplatte'

good host plants

SPRING-FLOWERING SHRUBS & CLIMBERS
Amelanchier, Ceanothus, Cotoneaster, Exochorda, Magnolia, Philadelphus, Spiraea, Syringa, Viburnum, Wisteria

SUMMER-FLOWERING SHRUBS
Buddleja, Ceanothus, Hydrangea paniculata and H. villosa
Shrub, rambler and climbing roses

EVERGREEN FOLIAGE SHRUBS
Buxus, Ilex, Osmanthus, Prunus lusitanica, Rhododendron, Taxus

SILVER-LEAVED SHRUBS
Elaeagnus angustifolia, E. 'Quicksilver', Hippophae rhamnoides, Pyrus salicifolia 'Pendula', Salix exigua

PURPLE-LEAVED SHRUBS
Berberis (all large purple forms), Cercis canadensis 'Forest Pansy', Cotinus 'Royal Purple', Rosa glauca (especially if coppiced)

GOLD-LEAVED SHRUBS
Catalpa bignonioides 'Aurea' (if pollarded), Cornus alba 'Aurea', Philadelphus coronarius 'Aureus'

VARIEGATED SHRUBS
Cornus alba 'Elegantissima', Cornus alternifolia 'Variegata', Rhamnus alaternus 'Variegata'

BERRYING SHRUBS TO COMBINE WITH CLEMATIS SEEDHEADS
Cotoneaster, Callicarpa, Euonymus europeaus 'Red Cascade', Malus 'Red Sentinel'

clematis for trees

Alpinas, macropetalas and strong-growing large-flowered hybrids, especially into small trees like Sorbus, Malus, Ilex, Magnolia, Pyrus, Acer ginnala, clipped yews (Taxus)

Montanas for large conifers and broad-leaf trees, such as vigorous crab apples, and for smaller trees only if the clematis is pruned regularly

FURTHER READING

Chesshire, Charles, RHS Practical Guides: Clematis, Dorling Kindersley, 1999

Clematis International, Journals of the International Clematis Society since 1984

Evison, Raymond, The Gardener's Guide to Growing Clematis, David and Charles, 1998

Fisk, Jim, Success with Clematis, Nelson, 1962

Fretwell, Barry, Clematis, HarperCollins, 1989

Grey-Wilson, Christopher, Clematis, The Genus, Batsford, 2000

Johnson, Magnus, The Genus Clematis 1997, English translation 2001, M. Johnson's Plantskola AB

Leeds, Everett, Toomey, Mary, and Chesshire, Charles, Encyclopaedia of Clematis, Timber Press, 2001

Lloyd, Christopher and Bennett, T., Clematis, Viking, 1989 revised edition of 1977 edition published by Collins

Markham, Ernest, Clematis, Country Life, 1935

Matthews, Victoria, The International Clematis Register and Checklist, Royal Horticultural Society, 2002

Moore and Jackman, The Clematis as a Garden Flower, John Murray, 1872

Robinson, William, The Virgin's Bower, John Murray, 1912, facsimile limited edition available from the British Clematis Society

The Clematis, Journals of the British Clematis Society since 1990

Toomey, Mary, Clematis: A Care Manual, Hamlyn, 1999

USEFUL ADDRESSES

societies

British Clematis Society
Membership Secretary
Valentine Cottage
Newnham Road
Hook
Hampshire RG27 9AE
England
www.britishclematis.org.uk

International Clematis Society
Fiona Woolfenden
3, Cuthbert's Close
Cheshunt
Waltham Cross, EN7 5RB
England
www.clematisinternational.com
(there are many national branches)

American Clematis Society
PO Box 17085
Irvine
California 92623
USA

Pacific Northwest Clematis Society
8007 SW Locust
Portland
Oregon 97223
USA

Japan Clematis Society
1548 Hikawa cho
Soka City
Saitama 340-0034
Japan

Swedish Clematis Society
Ulf Svensson
Laxholmsbacken 114
127 42 Skarholmen
Sweden

Estonian Clematis Society
Mrs Kulvi Kaus
Mustamae tee 60
01108 Tallinn
Estonia

Finland Clematis Club
Timo Lofgren
Hannika 32A 02360 ESPOO
Finland

registrars

Victoria Matthews
RHS International Clematis
Registrar
13 Chatsworth Close
Market Deeping
Peterborough PE6 8AZ
England
rhsclemreg@aol.com

Wim Snoeijer
Vest 162
2801 TX Gouda
The Netherlands

gardens and national collections

national collections, UK

Guernsey Clematis Nursery
Domarie Vineries
Les Sauvages
St Sampson
Guernsey
Channel Islands GY2 4FD
(over 600 varieties and wholesale nursery)

M. Oviatt Ham
Ely House
Green Street
Willingham
Cambridgeshire CB4 5JA
(atragenes and wholesale nursery)

Robin Savill
2 Bury Cottages
Bury Road
Pleshey
Chelmsford
Essex CM3 1HB
(collection of viticellas and mail-order nursery)

Mike Brown
Clematis Corner
15 Plough Close
Shillingford
Oxfordshire OX10 7EX
(herbaceous clematis)

Mr and Mrs J. Hudson
The Mill
21 The Mill lane
Cannington
Bridgewater
Somerset TA5 2HB
(*C. texensis* and cultivars)

open gardens, UK

Great Dixter
Northiam
Rye
East Sussex TN31 6PH
(gardens, nursery and mail order)

Burford House Gardens
Burford Garden Company
Tenbury Wells
Worcestershire WR15 8HQ
(also home of Treasures clematis nursery, retail and mail order, and national collection of over 300 varieties)

Sissinghurst Castle
Sissinghurst
Cranbrook
Kent TN 17 2AB

Stone House Cottage
Stone
Kidderminster
Worcestershire DY10 4BG
(gardens and nursery)

Sudeley Castle Gardens
Winchcombe
Gloucestershire GL54 5JD

Two gardens in asoociation with the British Clematis Society:

Bourne Hall Display Garden
Bourne Hall Park
Spring Street
Ewell
Surrey KT17 1UF

Helmsley Walled Garden
Cleveland Way
Helmsley
York
Yorkshire YO6 5AH

open gardens around the world

Estonia

Family Kivistik
Roogoja Talu
Karla kula
Kose 75101
Harjumaa
kivistik@trenet.ee
(also nursery)

Germany

Sachsische Landesanstalt fur
Landwirtschaft
Pillnitz Dresden

Klaus Korber
Gartenbauversuchsanstalt
D-97209 Veitshochheim
die.koerbers@t-online.de

Japan

Asamizo Park
Sagamihara City Green Assoc.
Asamizo-dai 2317-1
Sagamihara City
Kanagawa Prefecture 228

Sweden

Magnus Johnsson Collection
von Posts vag 1-3
SE-15139 Sodertalje

clematis nurseries

nurseries, England and Wales

T. H. Barker and Son
Baines Paddock Nursery
Haverthwaite
Ulverston
Cumbria LA12 8PF
(retail and mail order)

Beamish Clematis Nursery
Burntwood Cottage
Stoney Lane
Beamish
Co. Durham DH9 OSJ
(retail only)

J Bradshaw and Son
Busheyfields Nursery
Herne
Herne Bay
Kent CT6 7LJ
(retail, mail order)

County Park Nursery
Essex Gardens
Hornchurch
Essex RM11 3BU
(retail only, New Zealand clematis)

Crug Farm Plants
Griffiths Crossing
Near Caernarfon
Gwynedd LL55 1TU
Wales
(retail only, rare species)

The Hawthorns Nursery
Marsh Road
Hesketh Bank
Near Preston
Lancashire PR4 6XT
(retail and mail order)

Joe Link
Haybridge Nursery
Springacres
Dudnill
Cleobury Mortimer
Herefordshire DY14 ODH
(wholesale only)

New Leaf Plants
Amberley Farm
Cheltenham Road
Evesham
Worcestershire WR11 6LW
(wholesale only)

Paddocks Clematis Nursery
Sutton
Tenbury Wells
Worcestershire WR15 8RJ
(wholesale, retail and mail order)

Pennells Nursery
Newark Road
South Hykeham
Lincoln
Lincolnshire LN6 9NT
(retail only)

Peveril Clematis Nursery
Christow
Exeter
Devon EX6 7NG
(retail only)

The Plantsman Nursery
North Wonson Farm
Throwleigh
Devon EX20 2JA
(mail order, rare species)

Priorswood Clematis
Widbury Hill
Ware
Herts SG12 7QH
(retail and mail order)

Sheila Chapman Clematis
Crowther Nurseries
Ongar Road
Abridge
Essex RM4 1AA
(retail and mail order)

Taylors Clematis Nursery
Sutton Road
Sutton
Near Askern
Doncaster
South Yorkshire DN6 9JZ
(mail order only)

Thorncroft Clematis Nursery
The Lings
Reymerston
Norwich
Norfolk NR9 4QG
(retail, mail order and display gardens)

Woodcote Park Nursery
Ripley Road
Send
Woking
Surrey
(wholesale, retail and gardens)

nurseries around the world

Australia
Clematis Cottage Nursery
41 Main Street
Sheffield 7306
Tasmania

Austria
Jungpflanzenbaumschule
Alexander mittermayr
Griesbach
A-4770 Andorf

Canada
Skinner Nurseries
Box 220
Roblin
Manitoba ROL 1P0

Zubrowski, Stanley
PO Box 26
Prairie River
Saskatchewan SOE 1J0

Denmark
Flemming, Hansen
Solbakken 22
Ugelbolle DK 8410 Ronde

Finland
Puuterhakeskus Sofianletho
Sofianlehdonkatu 12
00610 Helsinki

France
Ellebore
La Chamotière
61360 St Jouin de Blavou

Le Jardin des Clematites
5 bis allée du Fond du Val, BP 172
76135 Mont St Aignan

Pépinière Botanique
Jean Thoby
Château de Gaujacq
40330 Amou

Travers
Cour Charette
45650 St Jean Le Blanc

Germany
Baumschul-Center Schmidtlein
Oberer Buhl 18
91090 Effeltrich

Friedrich Manfred Westphal
Peiner Hof 7
D-25497 Prisdorf

Wilhelm Kruse
Clematisgartnerei
Wallenbruckerstrasse 14
49328 Melle 7

Klaus Munster
Baumschulen
Bullendorf 19-20
25335 Altenmoor

Lothar Sachs
Clematisgartnerei
Grobstuckweg 10
01445 Radebeul

Adrian Straver
Gartenbau, Zum Waldkreus 97
46446 Emmerich Elte

Holland
Rein en Mark Bulk
Rjineveld 115
2771 XV Boskoop

Bulkyard Plants
PO Box 56
2779 AB Boskoop

Fa. C. Esveld
Rijneveld 72
2771 XS Boskoop

Henk J.M. Kuijf
Mennonietenbuurt 116A
1427BC Uithoorn

Ruud van der Werf
Lansing 23
2771 BK Boskoop

Ed Westerhoud
Boomwekerijen
Reijerskoop 305a
2771 BL Boskoop

Jan van Zoest
Azalealaan 29
2771 ZX Boskoop

Pieter G.Zwijnenburg Jr
Halve Raak 18
2771 AD Boskoop

Japan
Hayakawa Engei
65, Nakahongo Isumi Cho
Anjo City
Aicha Prefecture 444-1221

Shonan Clematis Nursery
3-7-24 Tsuzido-Motomachi
Fujisawa City
Kanagawa Prefecture 247-0043

New Zealand
Cadsonbury Plant Breeders
28 Vardon Crescent
Christchurch 8006

M. L. Jerard and Company
Potters Lane
Lansdowne Valley, RD2
Christchurch 8021

Poland
Ssczepan Marczynski
Szkolka Pojemnikowa
ul. Duchnicka 25
05-800 Pruszkow

Sweden
Cedergren and Company
Plantskola
Box 16016
250 16 Raa

Switzerland
Forster, Alfred
CH-3207 Golate

USA
Chalk Hill Clematis Farm
PO Box 1847
11720 Chalk Hill Road
Healdsburg
California 95448

Completely Clematis Specialty
  Nursery
217 Argilla Road
Ipswich
MA 01938

Donahues Greenhouses Inc.
420 10th Street SW
PO Box 366
Faribault
MN 55021
(wholesale only)

Heronswood Nursery
7530 NE 288th street
Kingston
Washington 98346

Joy Creek Nursery
20300 NW Watson Road
Scappoose
Oregon 97056

Klemm's Song Sparrow Farm
13101 East Rye Road
Avalon
Wisconsin 53505

Wayside Gardens
1 Garden Lane
Hodges
South Carolina 29695

INDEX

Species are listed under *Clematis* while hybrids and cultivars are listed under their own names

Page numbers in *italic* refer to the illustrations and captions

AUTHOR'S ACKNOWLEDGMENTS

Many thanks to all at Quadrille for making this book such a pleasure to create, especially Jane O' Shea, Carole McGlynn and Paul Welti. I am also grateful to Susanne Mitchell of the RHS for having faith in me. At home, untold thanks are due for the loving and patient encouragement of my wife Anne, who also checked and made sense of much of the text before it reached the publisher.

For my love of clematis, I must thank the late John Treasure who nurtured the enthusiasm of so many gardeners for this genus and whose beautiful garden at Burford House has always been a great inspiration to me. I would like to thank Yoki Aihara from Tokyo for organizing my trip to see wild clematis in the mountains of Honshu, and for showing me just how crazy one can be about a single genus.

My gratitude is also due to all those in clematis nurseries and enthusiasts up and down the country and around the world (you know who you are) for being so free in their knowledge and exchange of plants.

It was an inspiration to work with two great photographers, Andrew Lawson and Sarah Cuttle, who were encouraging about my own more modest efforts. Thanks also go to Jane and Brian Greetham for the loan of plants and for allowing us to use their nursery for some of our photographic shoots.

PHOTOGRAPHIC ACKNOWLEDGMENTS
The publishers thank those who have contributed photographs to this book. All photographs are by Andrew Lawson except those by Sarah Cuttle (38 below; 122;134-37; 139; 141-53), Charles Chesshire (1; 10; 11 right;18-19; 22-23; 31 below left; 37 below left & right; 39; 47 above; 58; 66-67; 73; 76; 77 below; 79; 82 below; 83; 84 left; 85; 88; 89 above; 91 above; 112 below; 116; 118; 120 below; 122 below; 132; 138; 139 left; 140) and Raymond J. Evison (107 below left;128 below).